GREG LEMOND'S Pocket Guide to BICYCLE MAINTENANCE AND REPAIR

GREG LEMOND

A Perigee Book

Perigee Books
are published by
The Putnam Publishing Group
200 Madison Avenue
New York, NY 10016

Library of Congress Cataloging-in-Publication Data

LeMond, Greg.
    [Pocket guide to bicycle maintenance and repair]
    Greg LeMond's pocket guide to bicycle maintenance and repair/
  by Greg LeMond.
        p. cm.
    The text on bicycle maintenance is taken from the Greg
LeMond's complete book of bicycling.
    ISBN 0-399-51511-9
    1. Bicycles—Maintenance and repair—Handbooks, manuals, etc.
I. Title.
TL430.L45   1990   89-38773 CIP
629.28′772—dc20

Printed in the United States of America
1 2 3 4 5 6 7 8 9 10

This book has been printed on acid-free paper.

Acknowledgments

Since winning the Tour de France, I have often been asked:
"What went through your mind before Laurent Fignon finished
the course?" Frankly, I can't remember. My only memory is
hearing French television commentator Jean-Paul Olivier tell me,
"Greg, tu as gagné. Greg, tu as gagné." He was telling me I
had won a Tour de France that, three weeks earlier, I was unsure
I could finish.

I had won my first Tour de France three years earlier, but
because of a bitter feud with my teammate Bernard Hinault, the
French press accused me of "stealing" that victory from him.
Although it should have been the highest moment of my career,
it was, paradoxically, in some respects the lowest.

Winning the 1989 Tour de France was entirely different. I
had returned from the abyss of a shooting incident, a bout with
appendicitis and, later, tendinitis. I hadn't won a bicycle race in
three years. Whenever I felt I was turning a corner, a new calamity appeared, and I often felt like quitting and settling down
to an ordinary life. So winning the Tour was unexpected, to say
the least, and greatly satisfying.

In those three years I could count on one hand the people
who believed in me. First and foremost among them was my
wife, Kathy. While she's shared the best moments of my career
with me, she's also been privy to my deepest personal desper-
ation. Without her great patience, courage, and love I don't think
I could have returned to the limelight.

As close to me in the hard times were my parents, Bob and
Bertha LeMond. I can imagine how difficult it must have been
for them to see me injured and unable to regain my talent.

Most of all, I'd like to acknowledge Pat Blades, my brother-
in-law, who is unfortunately notorious for having been the one
who accidentally pulled the trigger the day I was shot. Although

I never entertained for an instant the thought that Pat was to blame, I'm sure he must have felt guilty. Today, I owe something to Pat; his example of strength and dignity was a source of motivation.

Let me acknowledge Roger Scholl, who originally came up with the idea for this manual, and had the strength to sell the publisher on the concept. Let me also thank Lindley Boegehold and her enterprising and engaging assistant, Tina Isaac, who saw that Roger's idea was flawlessly executed.

CONTENTS

INTRODUCTION

As a professional cyclist, I have a small army of mechanics following me around the world. Every night they completely overhaul my bicycle, and during the races they do everything from changing wheels to replacing a broken seat post.

But even a professional cyclist has to do some of his own maintenance. After all, I train many hours a day away from my team, in the off-season, and in between races.

Just like any other cyclist, I have often experienced the frustration of getting a flat tire many miles from home, or having a brake rub irritatingly against the wheel. At some point or another, I have had to learn how to deal with practically any problem one can encounter riding a bicycle.

Countless cyclists have mentioned the need for a concise and easy-to-read explanation of the most common cycling problems—and how to fix them. I discovered that while there are a number of hefty desktop books on bicycle maintenance, there are almost no portable, easy-to-use formats that you can pack with you while riding. That is why I decided to write this pocket guide.

Most bicycle-repair problems can be easily fixed with a few basic tools you can carry with you. Only on rare occasions will you encounter a malfunction so grave that nothing can be done on the road. In fact, in the fifteen years that I have been a competitive cyclist, sometimes riding as much as eight hours a day, I have almost never been stuck with a broken part that forced me to scuttle a ride.

The first part of this guide deals with these common on-the-road cycling problems and explains how to correct them. The second half deals with routine maintenance you should do at home to avoid problems on the road. Some problems, such as flat tires, cannot be avoided through preventive maintenance. But many adjustments are easily managed at home in the space of a few minutes, so that later your bike is in shape to handle the hazards of the road.

Cycling is tremendous fun and is also one of the healthiest forms of exercise around. There is no reason to let a few mechanical problems get in the way of your enjoyment. The concise, to-the-point format of this pocket guide and the basic maintenance tips will help you deal with the vast majority of roadside repairs and get you quickly back in the saddle.

—Greg LeMond

1
ON-THE-ROAD REPAIRS

TOOLS

First, let's concentrate on the tools you can realistically pack with you on the road. The major limitations are obviously space and weight. A bulky tool like the bottom bracket fixed cup remover (if you have no idea what that means, relax, you don't really need to know) could never be carried easily on a bicycle: it's thirty inches long and weighs five or ten pounds.

Most of the repairs you will do on the road will involve replacing a spare tire (the most common repair), or adjusting brakes or derailleurs.

Here is the basic list of tools you should carry while riding:

Tools to carry with you on the road (clockwise from left): a spare sew-up or tubular tire, a Phillips-head and regular flat screwdriver, a nylon tool bag, a set of allen keys, a spare inner tube for a clincher tire, a set of tire irons, a spoke wrench, a quarter (for an emergency phone call), a set of flat wrenches, a three-way wrench, and a chain-rivet extractor.

1. *Three-way wrench* (also known as a T-wrench). This tool is a three-in-one wrench that features eight-, nine-, and ten-millimeter wrench sockets in one unit. On most bicycles, nearly every nut and bolt will be of either eight or ten millimeters. This tool is used to adjust brakes, brake levers, derailleurs, toe clips, and in some cases the seat-post bolt (the bolt that holds the seat post in the frame). There are some situations where you won't need this tool. If you have a low-priced American bicycle that features American-standard nuts and bolts, the metric three-way wrench won't fit; you'll need sockets that will fit American bolt sizes, measured in fractions of inches. The most common sizes are 8, 10, or 12 millimeter.

2. *Set of allen wrenches* (also called hex-head wrenches). These are small, L-shaped tools with six-sided (hence the moniker) hex heads. They are usually sold in a set of six or eight wrenches held on a ring or clamp. Allen wrenches are important, wonderfully compact tools used on all better bicycles built since the mid-seventies. They adjust derailleurs, the handlebar stem, seat-post bolt, and, in some cases, brakes and brake levers.

Important: If you decide to purchase these tools anywhere else than a bike shop (or if you have an old set lying about), be sure they fit your bicycle's components. Remember, most bikes have metric accessories; many auto-parts shops sell American-standard allen wrenches, which will not fit your metric components.

3. *A small flat-blade and/or Phillips-head screwdriver:* You need a screwdriver with a head small enough to fit into the stop screws that adjust your front and rear derailleurs. (Test the size of the screwdriver by trying it on the derailleur stop screws. See pages 89–90 for a discussion of derailleurs.) In addition, you may need a flat-blade screwdriver to tighten the small aluminum clamps that hold the brake cable to the top tube. (On most modern bicycles, however, that cable is held by small loops, built into the top tube, that require no adjustment.) *Important:* In some cases, derailleur stop screws are adjusted with a Phillips-head screwdriver. Check your derailleurs to determine which screwdriver you need. Of course, if you have components that

require both flat-blade and Phillips-head screwdrivers, you should carry both.

4. *Spoke wrench:* Used to tighten the spokes on your wheels. The most useful spoke wrench has multiple slats to accommodate a variety of different spoke-nipple sizes. (The spoke nipple is the ''bolt'' that fits into the rim of the wheel and screws into the spoke. The nipple is tightened to adjust, or ''true,'' the wheel.) The spoke wrench is inexpensive and lightweight. It can be surprisingly useful, as loose spokes are a common complaint.

5. *Chain-rivet tool:* This is used to remove a rivet from its link in the chain. The same tool is used to replace the rivet. This tool isn't needed frequently, usually only in cases where you've damaged one or two links of your chain in a minor accident, but it's relatively small, light, and inexpensive.

6. *Flat wrenches:* So called because they are wafer-thin, they are used on the road to adjust brakes that have become misaligned. A thirteen-millimeter flat wrench is used to adjust most better-quality bicycle brakes. A fifteen-millimeter flat wrench can come in handy if you need to remove your pedals. (*Caution:* An actual fifteen-millimeter pedal wrench is about twenty-four inches long and weighs three pounds, and provides you with much better leverage. The flat wrench will require a great deal more elbow grease. Some cyclists may find it impossible to remove pedals with a flat wrench. But for most it's an acceptable compromise, because a pedal wrench is too bulky to carry on the road.)

7. *Tire irons:* You will need these if you have clincher tires. If you have sew-up (or tubular) tires, you won't need tire irons. Tire irons are used to remove the clincher tire to allow you to replace or repair the inner tube.

8a. *Spare inner tube:* Again, this is necessary only if you have clincher tires. (If you have sew-ups, skip this item entirely and go to 8b.) It's one of the most important items to carry with you, since flat tires are a chronic cycling problem and there is little or no preventive maintenance to avoid them. Make sure you have the right inner-tube size, since size varies according to the type of clincher wheel you have.

8b. *Spare tire:* If you have sew-up tires, you will need to bring along a spare tire in the event of a flat. All sew-ups are one size (except for the rare twenty-four-inch-wheel sew-up for children's bikes), but prices vary tremendously. I recommend the inexpensive variety for most rides. Save expensive sew-ups for racing only.

9. *Frame pump.* This should fit your frame exactly.

A frame pump. This essential accessory should fit exactly your frame size.

10. *Spare roll of handlebar tape:* This can be useful in unexpected ways. For example, if you break a spoke on the freewheel side of your rear wheel, there is no way to remove the broken spoke without first removing the freewheel; use the handlebar tape to secure the stray spoke to a neighboring one.

11. *A quarter:* The last line of defense in roadside repair is a quarter to make a phone call to home or friends. It is rare that you will break a running part and find it impossible to continue, but if you do, you won't be able to fix your bike on the road. You can dispense with the quarter if you have a telephone credit card. Better yet, I recommend taking at least a few dollars to buy food and drinks—or get a cab ride, if need be.

12. *The seat bag for tools:* Once you have assembled the tools you will carry with you, you will need a convenient way to carry them. A number of manufacturers produce nylon bags that fit underneath the seat, specifically made to carry tools. Purchase the smallest bag that will carry the tools you need.

The tool set described above is a typical, complete road kit for the majority of modern bikes. By no means will these tools handle every conceivable repair. You can eliminate a number of the tools described above for short trips, and if your bicycle has a different design, some of the tools listed above will be unnecessary. (For example, I recommend bringing a flat wrench to remove pedals; some modern pedals have an allen-head bolt on the inside of the crankarm side.) On some bikes, you may need additional tools. Some seat posts, for example, require a twelve-millimeter socket wrench.

If you're planning a long touring trip with at least one night on the road, you should plan to carry a freewheel remover, some derailleur cable, some brake-cable housing, a piece of cable housing for the rear derailleur, some extra spokes (you can tape them to the top tube), and a wire cutter. It is impossible to list every tool you might need for such a trip, but the following checklist may help determine which tools you will most likely need. This list contains the tools most commonly used to adjust the bicycle components described. The choice of tools is listed in order, the most common tool first. These tools are those you can carry with you on the road to do emergency roadside repairs; major repairs are not taken into account here.

PART	TOOL
1. seat-post bolt holding seat	allen wrench or socket wrench
2. seat-post bolt in frame	allen wrench or three-way wrench
3. handlebar-stem bolt to frame	allen wrench or three-way wrench
4. handlebar-stem bolt to handlebars	allen wrench or three-way wrench
5. brake-levers bolt	three-way wrench, screwdriver or allen wrench
6. brake adjustment (if rubbing against wheel)	thirteen-millimeter flat wrench or allen wrench
7. brake-cable bolt (holding cable to brake)	three-way wrench or allen wrench
8. brake-shoe bolt (holding brake shoe to main brake body)	three-way wrench
9. front-derailleur clamp (holding front derailleur to frame)	three-way wrench or allen wrench
10. front-derailleur stop screws	flat-blade or Phillips screwdriver or allen head wrench
11. front-derailleur cable bolt (holds cable to front derailleur)	three-way wrench or allen wrench
12. chainring bolts (holds chainrings to crankarm)	allen wrench
13. pedals (axle holding pedal in crankarm)	fifteen-millimeter flat wrench or allen wrench
14. toe-clip nuts and bolts	three-way wrench
15. chain rivets	chain-rivet tool

16. rear-derailleur bolt (holds rear derailleur to frame) — allen wrench or three-way wrench
17. rear-derailleur stop screws — flat-blade or Phillips screwdriver or allen wrench
18. rear-derailleur cable bolt (holds cable to rear derailleur) — three-way wrench
19. spoke nipples — spoke wrench
20. clincher tire replacement (not necessary if you have sew-ups) — two tire irons
21. wheels fastened to bicycle with nuts (most bikes have quick release skewers or wing nuts) — two socket wrenches (sizes vary)

SAFETY

Cycling is an exhilarating sport. But it can also be dangerous. Balancing on two wheels, speeding down steep hills, and riding on wet roads are situations fraught with potential hazards. However, the great majority of cycling accidents involve cars. Sometimes such accidents are the cyclist's fault; more often, they're the fault of the automobile driver.

A cyclist must be forever wary because he is nearly always sharing the road with cars, other cyclists, and pedestrians. A cyclist cannot assume that a driver is alert. Thus the cyclist himself must be alert. If you see a car with its left-hand turn signal blinking, wait to see if the car makes a move; don't anticipate the car's turn—the turn signal might have been left on through sheer inattention. Similarly, a vehicle may turn without any signal at all; don't assume the car will continue in a predictable manner. You must be cautious, because in a collision with a two-thousand-pound vehicle, it doesn't take a genius to figure out who wins and who loses.

To protect yourself, *always* wear a helmet. In the old days, most cyclists wore a soft helmet known as a hair net (if they wore one at all). The hair net consisted of three link-sausage strips of foam wrapped in leather. In a crash, it was really no protection at all. The hardshell helmet, on the other hand, has a shock-resistant hard-plastic shell that meets the American National Standards Institute (ANSI) safety standards. Cycling helmets are surprisingly light and comfortable—and inexpensive. If you don't already own a helmet, get one before you go out riding again—and use it—. Your life could depend on it. Some cyclists refuse to wear a helmet because they think helmets don't look ''cool.'' But believe me, in the case of a crash, the alternatives (head injury, brain damage, or worse) far outweigh any whim of fashion.

There is a new product on the market called the ultralightweight hardshell helmet, made of a polystyrene shell. These helmets are remarkably light; some models weigh only seven ounces. They are also streamlined and can look quite ''cool.'' Most racers (who now have to wear helmets in the United States) have chosen ultralightweights. I like the ultralightweight made by Giro so much that I wear one even when I don't have to.

However, there is a real difference between an ultralightweight and a regular hardshell helmet. The ultralightweight is essentially only the polystyrene shell of the hardshell without the heavier, bulkier plastic bowl on the outside. This means the ultralightweight helmet is far lighter and sleeker. But it also means that once it's been subjected to any kind of impact, its structural strength is suspect. Ideally, you should buy a new one. Also, the ultralightweights are meant to protect the wearer in most collisions but not against the impact of a piercing object specifically.

I recommend ultralightweight helmets for experienced riders who have excellent bike-handling skills and who ride long hours. In fact, the ultralightweight is likely the best choice for most cyclists, except perhaps those who are not experienced and feel unsure about their ability to handle a bicycle. For these cyclists, I think a normal hardshell helmet is a wiser purchase.

Some cyclists might question my endorsement of helmets. Pro cyclists, it is often pointed out, almost never wear helmets, and when they do it's the hair-net variety, which gives little protection. While it's hard to argue with that, I'm proud to say that I was one of the first pros on the European circuit to wear an ultralightweight helmet, and I will continue to wear one in any situation I deem risky. I picked the model made by Giro, and I think it affords excellent protection. Remember, professional cyclists don't have to share the racecourse with automobiles. Riding on the open road in traffic is the most hazardous situation any cyclist can face.

The point is that the ultralightweight is an excellent choice for many cyclists: it affords real protection (most models meet ANSI safety standards), it is much lighter than the hardshell, and it is therefore less tiring. If your ultralightweight receives a significant jarring, you should consider replacing it. After all, what's more important—a few dollars or your head?

FIXING A FLAT TIRE

It's a beautiful weekend afternoon, and you're riding in the country, miles from home. Suddenly, you hear a disconcerting pop from your rear tire, followed by a high-toned hiss as the air escapes through a tear. You've had a flat.

The flat tire is the common cold of cycling. It is the most prevalent cycling problem and, unfortunately, there is no preventive cure. It can, however, be fixed in less time than you may think.

Replacing a Clincher Tire Inner Tube

The vast majority of bicycles sold today have clincher tires. The clincher is so called because the rubber tire clinches against the inner lips of the wheel's rim. An inflatable rubber inner tube inside the tire keeps the tire taut. In this respect, clinchers are similar to the old-style automobile tires.

When a clincher tire has a flat, it is the inner tube that is damaged, not the outside tire. Very rarely will you need to replace the tire itself (usually only if you damage it against a sharp piece of glass or a rock). Even if the tire is damaged, you can usually keep riding as long as the inner tube is intact. Only a major tear in the tire itself would force you to have to replace it.

As I mentioned before, if you have clincher tires, always carry a spare inner tube and a set of tire irons. You may want to carry a patch kit as well. While some cyclists believe that punctured inner tubes should be fixed at all costs, I believe that repairs take too long (usually at least fifteen minutes) and are usually successful only briefly.

Since inner tubes are inexpensive and patch kits not much cheaper, I don't think patching an inner tube (especially on the road) is worthwhile.

To replace a damaged inner tube, first remove the wheel from the frame. If your flat is on the front wheel, this is a relatively simple process. First, loosen the tension lever on the brakes. This opens up the brakes slightly to let the wheel slide through. On some bikes, the tension lever can be found by the top of the brake caliper where the cable housing joins the brake arms. Loosening the brake with the tension lever can be especially important if you have thick clinchers (this applies most of all to any bike with fat tires). Some less-expensive brakes have a tension lever on the brake levers themselves, in the form of a clamp that lifts and loosens the brake lever to open the brakes.

Next, loosen the hub bolts holding the hub to the bicycle forks. Most bicycles today have a quick-release mechanism. This device is a slightly curved arm, about two inches long, holding the wheel in place. To loosen it, open the arm and let the wheel drop out. (You may have to turn the quick-release arm a few times while holding the cone-shaped nut on the other side in place.)

Some less-expensive bikes use wing nuts to fasten the wheels to the fork. These are propeller-shaped nuts that can be removed without a wrench by simply turning them counterclockwise.

On the least-expensive bicycles, the wheels are held in place by simple nuts. Removing these wheels usually requires two large wrenches (sizes vary). If you have a bike with these nuts, I recommend replacing them with wing nuts, which can fit on any wheel that features simple nuts. Better yet, you could get quick-release skewers; but that would involve buying a new set of hubs, because the quick-release skewers require a special hub construction.

Unfastening the rear wheel is a bit more involved; the free-wheel, chain, and rear derailleur hold the wheel firmly in place.

The first step, as with the front wheel, is to loosen the tension lever on the rear brake to open a space wide enough so that the wheel may slide through. Next, unfasten the quick-release skewer, wing nuts, or nuts holding the wheel to the bicycle frame. You'll probably find that the rear wheel resists sliding off the frame. This is because of the tension exerted by the chain, which acts to hold the freewheel in place.

To overcome this, position yourself behind the bike and pull back on the rear derailleur with your right hand. This should serve to free the chain from the freewheel. You should now be

Removing the rear wheel. From behind the bike, grasp the rear derailleur in your right hand.

When you've pulled back on the rear derailleur as far as possible, push the wheel forward and down to dislodge it.

able to slide the wheel out of the frame stays. If the wheel still refuses to be dislodged, give the top of the wheel a firm push with your left hand.

It might take a bit of yanking and tugging, but the wheel should slide out without too much difficulty. Don't bang or force the wheel, though, as you might damage it. If the wheel doesn't come off relatively easily, try loosening the brakes or wheel nuts some more.

Once the wheel is removed, take out the two tire irons and the spare inner tube from your tool kit. Place the first tire iron under the lip of the rim, where the tire meets the rim. Slide and wiggle it carefully under the lip (never force it—you may damage the tire itself). With one end of the tire iron under the lip, the length of the tire iron sticking out should be parallel with the spokes of the wheel. You'll notice a notch or crescent-shaped hole on the arm of the tire iron. Use this hole to anchor the tire iron by securing it to a spoke. With the first tire iron in place, the edge of the tire should be sticking out of the rim.

Next, insert the second tire iron under the rim near the first tire iron. Begin sliding it slowly around the circumference of the wheel, dislodging the clincher tire from the rim of the wheel. After you've finished, one side of the tire will be free of the lip of the wheel's rim.

Removing a clincher tire. Slide the first tire iron (the one pictured on the left) under the lip of the tire and anchor it to a spoke, as shown. Next, insert the second tire iron and gently slide it away from the first tire iron to dislodge the tire from the rim.

Remove both tire irons. To dislodge the other side of the tire (the one that's still resting inside the lip of the rim), take a single tire iron and insert it under the lip of the rim. Because the first side of the tire is free of the rim, dislodging the second side should be far easier. In fact, the other side should simply pop out so you can peel it off with your hands (or slide the tire iron around the circumference of the wheel) as you did with the other side).

This procedure becomes very easy with a little practice. I suggest you practice removing a tire from a wheel at home, so that you get the hang of it before you get stuck on the road.

With the tire off, you will see the deflated inner tube. Locate the valve and push it out of the rim of the wheel through the valve opening in the rim. (Some manufacturers place a ring around the inner-tube valve to prevent valve damage. This ring must be unscrewed before you can remove the valve.) Next, remove the inner tube from the rim. You can either discard the old inner tube or take it home to repair it (more on that below).

Unfold the new inner tube and pump it up slightly with your frame pump so that it is soft and squishy. Place the valve of the new inner tube into the valve hole in the rim and drape the

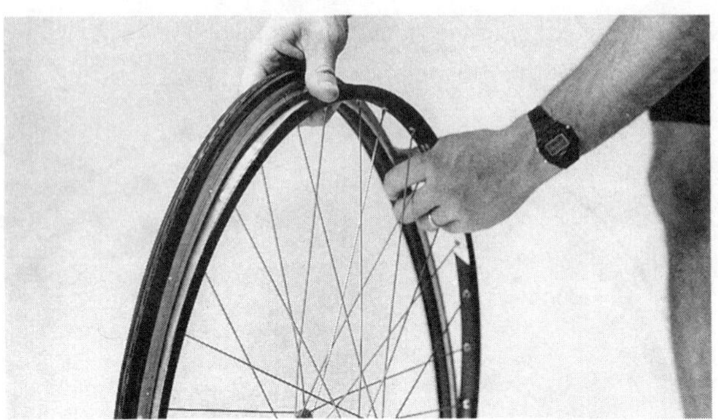

After you have dislodged one side of the tire from the rim, you should be able to easily remove the rest of the tire from the rim by hand.

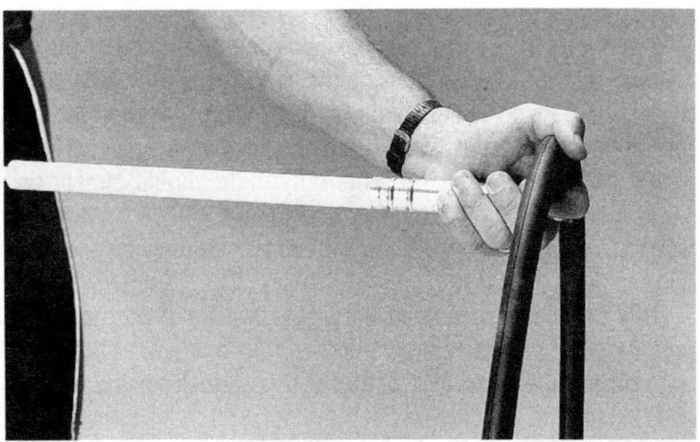

Next, pump enough air into the new inner tube so that it is slightly squishy. This will make it easier to work with.

inner tube around the rim. You might be surprised to discover that the inner tube seems too big for your wheel. But don't worry—that's how all new inner tubes look when they are installed.

Next, replace the tire over the inner tube. Take the tire and begin fitting it over the inner tube. (At this point, the inner tube

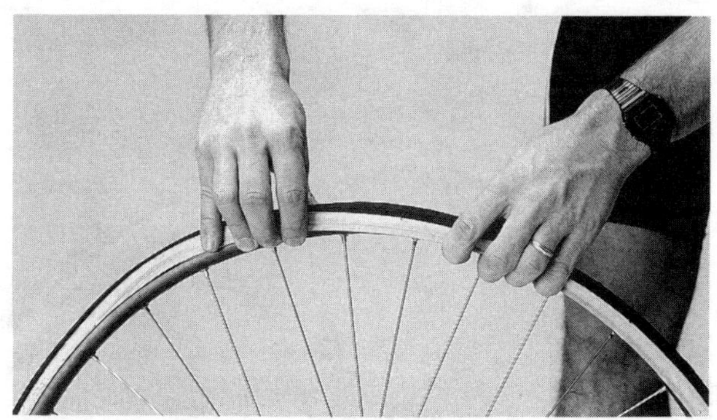

To replace the tire, place the inner tube on the rim and insert the tire into the lip of the rim by hand on one side.

is connected to the rim only by the valve.) When you get near the bottom, force the tire over the inner tube by hand, which should be fairly easy. Now you have an inner tube sitting on the rim and a tire sitting over the inner tube. But the tire has not yet been inserted inside the lip of the rim. And that's the hard part.

Begin inserting one side of the tire into the lip of the rim. You can do this by hand at first, by stuffing the tire bead (another word for tire) in the gap between the inner tube and the lip of the rim. Always begin at the valve stem (to ensure that you never use a tire iron near the valve, which is the most fragile part of the inner tube). You should be able to fit one side of the tire into the lip of the rim by hand (use the palm of your hand for extra force if you're having trouble getting the last bit of the tire bead over the rim). If necessary, use a tire iron to insert the last few inches of the tire wall. A word of caution: Use a tire iron on a new inner tube with great caution. A tire iron can easily puncture the inner tube. As much as possible, I try to avoid using a tire iron when installing a new inner tube.

Once you have gotten the first side of the tire into the lip of the rim, you must insert the other side. Push the tire in by hand, beginning with the valve stem. Depending on your dexterity and

Inserting the last few inches of the tire bead is difficult. You may want to use a tire iron, as shown here, although you must be careful not to puncture the inner tube. If you try to push the tire into the rim by hand, you will need a fair amount of strength.

strength, you may have to resort to using tire irons. Getting the last two to six inches inside the rim is the hard part.

There are two ways of getting this last part of the tire over the lip of the rim. The first is the biceps-and-quadriceps method, which requires little finesse and a bit of strength. The second method I call the forceps method, because it involves using tire irons.

To use the biceps-and-quadriceps method, take the wheel in your arms and hold the uncooperative section of the tire away from you. Cupping the wheel with your body and legs, apply force with your palms and hands until the tire pops in.

To use the forceps method, slide the tire iron under the tire at the beginning of the section of tire that remains outside the rim. Twist the tire iron until a section of the tire pops into place on the lip of the rim. At first, you'll find that this is a fairly easy maneuver—that is, until you reach the final two to four inches. At that point, the tire will tighten so much that you will be convinced that the laws of nature are against you. Continue twisting the tire iron, using your other hand to keep the portion of tire already in place from popping out as you finish the job.

With the tire properly in place, inflate the inner tube to the correct pressure. If you don't have a tire-pressure gauge, you can estimate the proper pressure by feeling the firmness of the tire. Then replace the wheel.

One final word about reinstalling wheels. Replacing a rear wheel can be challenging. But just remember the steps you followed to remove the rear wheel. Get behind the bike and slip the rear wheel into its cavity in between the chain stays. Pull the rear derailleur back as far as it will go with your right hand to get the chain properly around the freewheel. With your left hand (and some fingers of your right hand) gently rock or slide the wheel back toward you until the rear-wheel hub axle is properly seated in the slots (or dropouts, as they are called). Then tighten the hub locks, making sure the wheel is properly centered. Finally, close the brake release lever.

Occasionally, when removing or replacing a rear wheel, the chain may slip off the chainring (the big gear rings connected to the right pedal). If that happens, lift the chain by hand onto the small chainring. (You may have to push the front-derailleur lever—almost always the lever on the left side of the bike—as far toward the front as it will go.) Use a piece of cloth or a rag to wrap around your hands to avoid getting chain grease on them.

Occasionally, the chain will slip off the chainrings when you remove the rear wheel. To avoid this, place the chain on the small chainring.

FIFTEEN STEPS FOR REPLACING A CLINCHER TIRE

1. Loosen tension lever on brake.
2. Unfasten quick-release skewer, wing nuts, or nuts.
3. Remove wheel.
4. Insert first tire iron under lip of tire right above valve: anchor it to spoke.
5. Insert second tire iron under lip of tire, next to first tire iron; slide around rim, popping the tire out of the rim.
6. Place one tire iron under lip of tire on other side of wheel.
7. Slide tire iron all around rim on other side.
8. Remove tire. Set aside.
9. Remove inner tube.
10. Pump new inner tube slightly until soft and squishy.
11. Install new inner tube, seating valve in valve hole.
12. Fit tire over inner tube.
13. Insert tire into lip on one side.
14. Insert tire into lip on other side. Tire irons might be necessary at the end.
15. Inflate new inner tube to correct pressure rating, or until firm to the touch. Replace wheel on bike.

Repairing Inner Tubes

Some cyclists assert that knowing how to repair inner tubes is as necessary in cycling as pedaling and changing gears. By fixing their old tubes, they believe they are saving money. I disagree. I believe that it isn't worth your while to repair old inner tubes, especially since many patched inner tubes often puncture again at the patch.

But if you are on a long trip and you have no additional spare inner tubes, carry the damaged tube along. You may find that you will have to patch the inner tube if you get another flat. But be prepared to sit by the side of the road for a considerable time while you find the break (sometimes you need to submerge the inner tube in water to discover it) and then let the bonding compound dry. I also recommend canned sealers, which are a stopgap measure until you can purchase another inner tube.

To repair a punctured inner tube, you will need a patch kit. Patch kits are available at all bike shops. First, remove the inner tube (following the steps above) and locate the puncture. You may need to pump air into your inner tube with your frame pump to find the hole. If the hole is too small to locate by eye, you must pump a little air in the inner tube and submerge it in water. Air from the puncture will create bubbles, revealing its location.

Apply a few drops of the glue that is included in the patch kit and quickly place the patch over the puncture hole. Let it dry for at least fifteen minutes. Next, test the inner tube by inflating it to see that the patch is well bonded to the inner tube. Replace the inner tube and tire as above. You will need to release most of the air from the inner tube before replacing the tire on the rim.

Replacing a Sew-up Tire

Sew-up (or tubular) tires are found only on a small number of racing bicycles. Racers choose sew-ups because of the greater performance they provide and the ease in changing them on the road.

You might ask yourself why anybody would choose clincher tires if sew-ups perform better and are easier to change. But there is a catch. Sew-ups are far more expensive than clinchers and they puncture much more frequently. Sew-ups consist of one integral unit in which the tire—a tube made of woven cotton or silk fibers—is sewn around a thin inner tube (hence the name). So you must purchase an entire unit (not only an inner tube, as is the case with clinchers) to replace a flat on the road. You can buy an inexpensive sew-up for about fifteen dollars; some cost as much as eighty dollars. By comparison, a clincher inner tube costs about three dollars.

Sew-up inner tubes *can* be patched, but this requires carefully opening up the tire and sewing it up again. It is a job that requires specialized tools and much experience. It is something I can't recommend, because I've never been able to do it successfully.

Needless to say, it is crucial for you to carry at least one spare sew-up on any ride.

To carry a spare tire with you, you should first learn to fold it properly so that it will not be damaged. Place the tire on a flat surface and hold it by the valve. Spread the tire out so that the valve is protected in the middle. Fold the tire in three- to four-inch sections, making sure the valve is protected. You should end up with a compact package. Place the folded tire in a small plastic bag and place it in your seat pack or strap it under your seat with a spare toe strap (make sure the spare is kept away from tools that could puncture it).

To replace a flat tire, first remove the wheel (see the section above on clincher tires for the steps on removing a front and rear wheel).

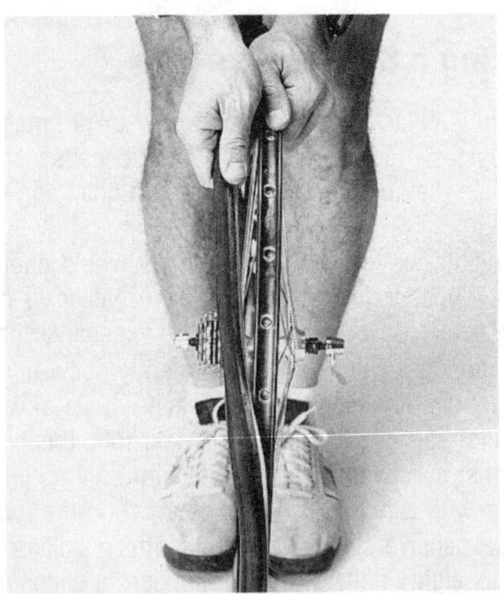

To remove a sew-up or tubular tire from the rim, you will have to literally tear it off the rim, to which it is bound by a special adhesive glue.

Once you've removed the wheel, dislodge the tire from the rim of the wheel. Sew-ups are bound to the rim by a special tire glue. To remove a sew-up, you must quite literally tear it off the rim. Place the wheel on the ground so that the valve is at the bottom of the wheel, facing up. Hold the wheel firmly with your legs. Grab a section of the tire near the top of the wheel and force the tire off the rim, pushing with your thumbs and forefingers. Continue pushing until the entire tire has been freed from the rim.

Sometimes a sew-up will come off without much effort. This usually means that the tire was poorly glued to the rim in the first place. And although it is certainly easier to remove, a poorly glued sew-up can be dangerous because it can roll off the rim on a sharp turn or after a long downhill (when the heat from the brakes can melt the tire glue). More commonly, you will find that removing a sew-up from the rim is a Herculean task.

Once the punctured tire is off the wheel, unfold the new tire. Before putting it on the rim, pump enough air so that the tire is soft and squishy. Then position the wheel so that the valve opening is at the top of the wheel. Place the valve of the tire in the valve opening. Grip the wheel with your legs and put the tire onto the rim, pulling down on the tire to stretch it out. When you get near the bottom of the wheel, raise the bottom of the

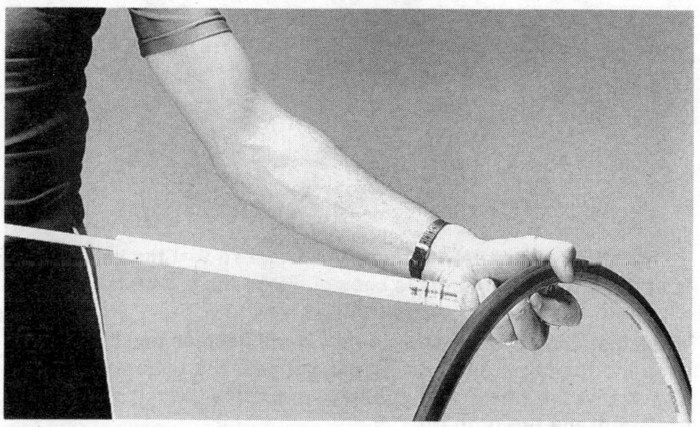

Before installing the spare sew-up on the rim, pump enough air into it so that it is soft and squishy, and easier to work with.

rim a few inches off the ground, using some force, and squeeze the last few inches of the tire onto the rim. With the tire on the rim, inflate the new sew-up to its maximum pressure. (A sew-up installed on the road without the benefit of glue and drying time should always be inflated to maximum pressure; this will ensure against rolling the tire in a curve.)

To install the spare sew-up, turn the wheel so that the valve hole is at the top of the wheel (as shown). Place the tire on the rim with both hands.

When installing a spare sew-up tire, it will become much harder to wrap the tire around the rim as you get near the bottom of the wheel. Cup the wheel with your legs and force the remaining portion of the tire onto the rim.

A spare sew-up installed on the road should always be applied *dry,* without glue. The tire is held to the rim by the pressure against the rim when the tire is inflated. In addition, the glue previously applied to the rim should be enough to get you home safely (as long as you ride cautiously). But too much glue applied to the rim will cake up and reduce the size of the lip of the rim.

A common mistake made by cyclists unfamiliar with sew-ups is to apply tire glue to the rim during a roadside tire change. This is an ill-advised tactic, because the glue won't have time to dry unless you can wait overnight. And wet glue is much worse than no glue at all, because the tire, without a firm surface for bonding, can roll off the wheel on a sharp curve.

If you have a rim with a build-up of tire glue from a number of previous tire changes, it won't require any additional glue (in fact, it is possible to have *too much* glue on a sew-up rim, in which case it must be cleaned with glue remover and new coats of fresh glue reapplied). Once you are home again, you should remove the replacement sew-up, add a little glue, and let it dry overnight, as I discuss below.

Applying Glue on Sew-ups at Home

There are two kinds of bicycle-tire glue. The first is a clear, thin liquid that quickly dries to form a cementlike bond between tire and rim that is so strong it sometimes is nearly impossible to remove the tire once you've had a flat. One would think this is the better glue because it forms a strong bond. But the problem with this glue is that once it dries it retains no adhesive qualities, which can be dangerous.

I recommend the clear variety of glue for cyclists who rarely or never need to change flats on the road—in other words, those cyclists who have the luxury of taking the wheel back to a workshop and applying a new coat of cement to the rim. Professional cyclists use it because they have team support cars with spare sets of wheels. This is a convenience the vast majority of riders don't have—including me, when I'm training on my own.

The second kind of glue is a burgundy-red goo that is infuriatingly sticky. It clings to any surface it touches and is nearly impossible to remove. This glue never completely dries. While it doesn't quite form the rock-perfect bond of the clear glue, the red goo can be used again and again on the road when replacing a flat sew-up. Because it remains gooey and sticky for months, this glue will form enough of a bond to hold a tire replaced on the road without any new glue being applied. It is still preferable to let the wheel sit overnight, even with glue already on the rim. Of course, once you get home, you should remove the replacement sew-up, add a little glue, and let the wheel sit overnight. The only exception to this rule is if you have a large buildup of glue on the rim, in which case you should remove the built-up glue with glue remover or paint remover and apply fresh glue.

After changing tires a few times, you may no longer need to apply any new glue. And although you will need to exercise some caution immediately after installing a spare sew-up on the road, in most cases there should be enough glue on the rim so that the tire will be securely bonded to the rim by the following morning. One note of caution, however: Even the sticky red goo eventually dries and loses its adhesive qualities; when it does, you will need to remove the old glue with glue remover (available at neighborhood bike shops) and apply fresh glue.

A common trick of the professional mechanic is to combine the clear cement and the burgundy-red goo into a mixture that is both sticky and cementlike. A simpler solution for the home practitioner who would like to avoid the awful mess of mixing glues is to apply a base of burgundy-red goo the first few times a spare tire is installed, then to begin using the clear adhesive in subsequent applications. Personally, I think this is necessary only if you need a very strong bond. Remember, when the clear bond dries, it will dry *over* the red goo, and the entire lot will then be dry and unable to form a bond with a replacement tire.

ON-THE-ROAD FLAT-TIRE MAINTENANCE

Whether you have clincher tires or sew-ups, the most effective on-the-road maintenance to prevent flat tires is to rub the surface of the tire as you ride, by placing a gloved hand lightly over the moving tire (*Important:* Be sure to wear gloves if you attempt this, as you may encounter sharp glass shreds or other objects that could cut your hand.) Brushing the tires in this fashion can help to dislodge any foreign objects that can puncture your tires.

EIGHT STEPS FOR REPLACING A SEW-UP TIRE

1. Loosen tension lever on brake.
2. Loosen quick-release skewer, wing nuts, or nuts.
3. Remove wheel (for rear wheel, pull back on rear derailleur to relieve the chain tension on the wheel).
4. Remove sew-up from rim, beginning at the point farthest from the valve (the valve portion of the wheel should be resting on the ground).
5. Pump new tire with a little air until it's soft and squishy.
6. Place tire-valve stem in the valve hole of the rim (with the wheel positioned so that the valve hole is at the top of the wheel).
7. Place the tire on the rim, using force to seat the last few inches of the tire on the rim surface.
8. Inflate sew-up to correct pressure.
Note: Ride with caution until the replacement tire bonds with the glue on the rim. If the rim does not have sufficient glue to hold the tire properly, ride with caution until you can apply new glue at home and let it dry overnight.

Repairing a Sew-up Tubular Tire

To patch a sew-up, purchase a patch kit (the same kind used for clincher tire inner tubes). You also need a tube of epoxy and a special set of sew-up needles, sew-up thread, and a pair of sewing or surgical scissors. The first step is to remove the cloth strip that protects the stitching of the sew-up. You can remove this strip by hand.

Next, carefully begin removing the stitches with the small sewing or surgical scissors. Unless you can immediately spot the location of the puncture, you will need to remove the stitching all the way around the sew-up; this usually takes about forty-five minutes.

Dislodge the inner tube and pump it up slightly with air. If you can't sight the puncture by air, you need to fill a sink with water and submerge the inner tube; fill the inner tube with air and squeeze it until you see bubbles escaping from the point of the puncture.

Next, apply the glue from the patch kit to the inner tube (taking care to thoroughly dry the inner tube if you dunked it in water). Place the patch and let it dry. If you have a high-quality sew-up, the rubber is often very slippery and you may have to place the patch a few times before it remains firmly glued.

The most difficult part of this procedure is closing the stitching, which involves working with the special sew-up needles and with sew-up thread or heavy-duty nylon thread. Make sure you pass the thread only through the original holes in the sew-up tire. For a professional mechanic, closing up a sew-up tire can take anywhere from forty-five minutes to several hours. For a novice, it could take longer.

To finish, glue the protective cloth strip to the resewn tire. Use epoxy sparingly to do this, making sure not to get any on your hands.

Let me further caution you that unless you're willing to go through this procedure a number of times, you probably won't be able to effectively fix a punctured sew-up. This is a procedure that takes a lot of experience, skill, and time. Most modern cyclists don't have the time that the great old-world mechanics do to learn this specialized skill.

BRAKE ADJUSTMENTS

It happens to every cyclist. One day, while on an exhilarating ride through the countryside, you notice a squeak, a little, irritating squeak coming from one of your wheels. Perhaps you notice that your wheel is dragging a bit. More likely than not, the explanation for the squeak, or the sudden resistance of the wheel, is that one of the brake shoes is rubbing against the rim of the wheel. This kind of rubbing is not caused by damage, but by misalignment. And misalignment is easily remedied on the road in just a few moments.

How did your brake get misaligned? Occasionally because of a crash, but more often the brakes fall out of alignment gradually under the stress of use.

First, take a look at the front and rear brakes to determine which one is rubbing against the wheel. Next, open your tool kit and remove the thirteen-millimeter flat wrench. (This tool will work for most brands of brakes. But there may be some exceptions, so check with your bicycle shop.) Most thirteen-millimeter

Brakes fall out of alignment under the rigors and stress of riding.

flat wrenches have a fourteen-millimeter opening on the opposite end; make sure you are using the correct end of the wrench.

Place the thirteen-millimeter flat wrench in the gap between the brake body (what you and I would call the brake: the metallic arms and levers) and the bicycle forks (for the front brake) or the bike-frame brake bridge (for the rear brake). Slowly turn the flat wrench in the appropriate direction to center the brake shoes in relation to the wheel. (For example, if the right side of the brake is rubbing against the wheel, turn the wrench to the left).

As you turn the wrench you should encounter some resistance—the brake should be quite difficult to turn. If the brake moves with little effort, then the entire brake body is not tightly installed on the frame. If this is the case, you will need to tighten the brake, a procedure described in the maintenance chapter on pages 94–100.

Many people adjust their brakes, put their wrench back into their tool kit, and continue riding—only to discover, the next time they use their brakes, that they have fallen out of alignment again.

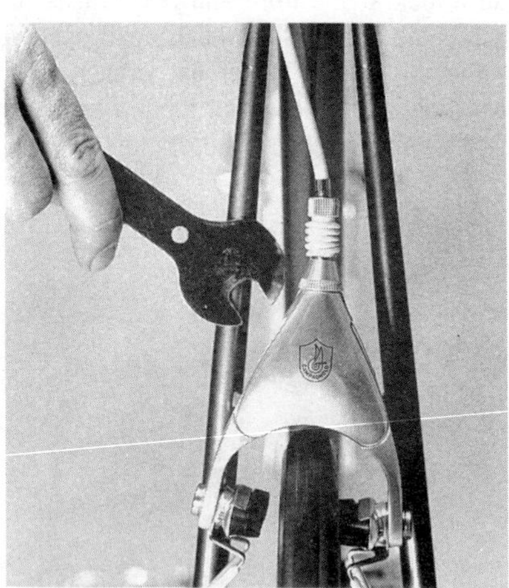

To align your brake, take out a thirteen-millimeter flat wrench from your tool kit and insert it in the "flat" between the brake body and the frame.

To center the brake, turn the thirteen-millimeter wrench in the opposite direction. You will need to overcompensate slightly. After you apply the brake lever once, check the position of the brakes again. If they are still slightly misaligned, fine tune the adjustment until they remain centered after applying the brakes.

To avoid this, overcompensate a bit when adjusting the brake shoes, beyond the point where the brake is centered and well adjusted, until it is slightly misaligned in the opposite direction. Now apply the brakes, giving the brake lever a good, firm squeeze. Look at the brake shoes. If the brake is still listing to the side it was rubbing on, you did not overcompensate enough. If, instead, it's now off center in the opposite direction, you overcompensated too much. Fine tune your adjustments until the brakes are perfectly centered after applying the brake lever.

Often, brakes fall out adjustment because the brake body has loosened under the stress of use (as described above). If your brake falls out of alignment regularly, tighten the brake body as explained in the maintenance chapter.

Perfectly adjusted brakes are usually the result of a little trial and error.

SEVEN STEPS TO BRAKE ADJUSTMENT

1. Check to see if the brake is rubbing, and if so, on which side.
2. Remove thirteen-millimeter flat wrench from tool-kit bag.
3. Insert flat wrench in gap between brake body and bicycle frame.
4a. Turn wrench to center brake (if left side of brake is rubbing, turn to right).
4b. If brake turns without effort, brake body is loose on bicycle frame. Refer to maintenance chapter (pages 100–103) for instructions on tightening the brake body.
5. Overcompensate your adjustment so that brake appears slightly off center in opposite direction.
6. Press brake lever firmly.
7. Inspect brake. If centered, brake is adjusted. If still off center, fine tune adjustment.

Brake-Cable Problems

One of the most serious problems you can encounter on the road is breaking a brake cable. Luckily, this is an extremely rare occurrence. If you are unfortunate enough to experience a broken brake-cable problem, stop as quickly as possible with the brake that still works.

The matter of replacing a brake cable begins before you leave home. Although different bikes require different lengths of cable housing (every bicycle is set up by hand and the cable housing cut individually, so the length of cable needed will vary in each case), all brake cable is sold in one length. The cable must be cut with a pair of wire cutters to fit your bike. Because wire cutters are heavy (and rarely needed), it isn't practical to bring them with you on the road. Instead, cut a replacement brake cable at home by removing the brake cable already installed in your brakes and placing it next to a new replacement cable. Then use the wire cutters to cut the replacement cable to the same length as the original cable. Reinstall the original cable (as described below). Roll up the replacement cable and place it in your tool bag to carry with you.

If you don't have a replacement cable with you and the rear brake cable breaks, you can continue riding safely until you reach a bike shop or home. But if you break the front brake cable, then you have lost about 80 percent of your braking power. You can ride safely only if you are on flat terrain. Riding downhill without the front brake is an invitation to disaster.

To replace a brake cable, first remove the severed cable. Take out the three-way wrench from your tool kit and loosen the bolt that holds the cable to the brake body. Once that portion of the severed cable is free, slide it out of the brake housing. The other portion of the split cable is now only loosely anchored in the brake lever (the handles attached to the handlebars that you squeeze to apply the brakes).

To release this second portion of the broken cable, open the brake lever as wide as it will go. Inside you will see the brake cable anchored to the brake lever by a device called the bar-

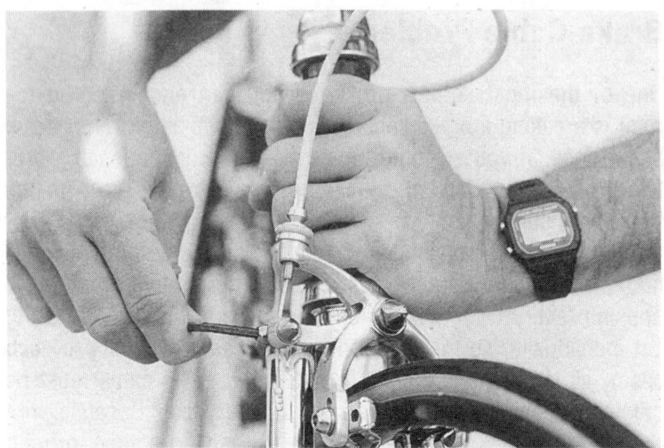

Removing a severed cable from the brake body. (*Note:* In the case of these C-Record Campagnolo brakes, an allen key is used to loosen the bolt that holds the brake cable to the brake body. But on most brakes, you will need a three-way wrench or an eight-millimeter wrench.)

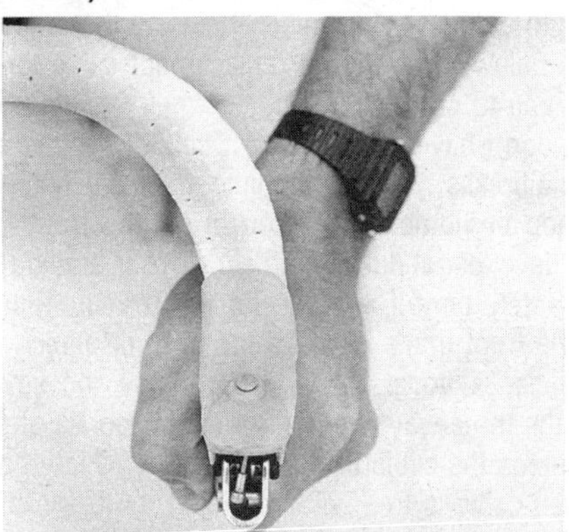

The barrel end of the brake cable, seated in the barrel lock. With the brake cable loosened, you should be able to slip the barrel end from its seat to remove the cable.

rel lock. Seated in this barrel lock is the barrel end of the brake cable. To remove it, grab the cable in one hand and the barrel lock with the other hand. Push the cable through the barrel lock.

Occasionally, this is quite easy. As soon as the barrel end is free, you can easily thread the rest of the cable through the barrel lock. More often, the barrel end has become embedded in its seat in the brake lever and requires a little force to be removed. This is not easy, because the cable buckles fairly easily. If the barrel end is firmly entrenched in the barrel lock, you may need the flat-blade screwdriver from your tool kit to tap the barrel end out of the brake lever.

To replace the brake cable, slide the cable through the barrel lock until the barrel end of the cable rests in the barrel lock (which is in the brake lever). When that end is firmly in place (it will have a tendency to slide out of place until the cable is secured and taut), slide the cable through the cable housing, then through to the bolt that holds the cable to the brake body.

This is where replacing a brake cable alone can get a little tricky. You need to (1) hold the brake shoes firmly against the wheel; (2) pull down on the cable to make sure it is fully taut; and (3) tighten the bolt that secures the cable. That makes three tasks for two hands. That's why there's a special tool for the job, called the third hand. This tool is a spring clamp designed to hold the brake shoes against the wheel while you pull down on the cable and tighten the cable bolt. Regrettably, the third hand, the Big Foot of cycling tools, is impractical to carry in most under-the-seat tool kits.

There is a solution for on-the-road repair. If you don't have someone with you who can hold the brake shoes against the rim, omit pulling the brake cable so that it's fully taut. Skipping this step means your new brake cable won't be quite as taut as it should be when you finish. But you will be able to hold the brake shoes firmly against the wheel with one hand (absolutely crucial) and tighten the cable in its bolt in the brake body with the other hand.

Once you've finished the job, you can further tighten the cable with the adjustable barrel. This device allows you to tighten the cable *after* you've fastened the cable onto the bolt. The adjustable barrel is most often found at the following locations: (1) at the top of the brake caliper (the brake body) where the brake ends and the cable housing begins; (2) next to the bolt that holds the cable to the brake body; or (3) at the top of the brake lever, where the brake lever ends and the cable housing begins. The adjustable barrel often looks like a rubber disc that turns along an inch-long barrel (or it may look like a ribbed metal barrel).

By gradually turning the adjustable barrel clockwise (or, as with some brakes, counterclockwise), you can take up the slack in the brake cable. *Note:* Be careful that your adjustable barrel is in its initial or starting position—with the maximum length of the barrel available to take up cable slack—when you tighten the cable bolt.

ELEVEN STEPS TO EMERGENCY BRAKE-CABLE REPLACEMENT

1. *At home:* Remove original brake cable (as described below).
2. Place original brake cable and replacement cable side by side, and use wire cutters to cut replacement cable same length as original cable.
3. Replace original cable (as described below).
1. *On the road:* Remove three-way wrench from tool-kit bag.
2. Loosen bolt holding brake cable to brake body.
3. Remove first portion of severed cable. Set aside.
4. Open brake lever widely.
5. Free barrel end of brake cable from brake lever.
6. Remove second portion of severed brake cable. Set aside.
7. Install new brake cable, placing barrel end in barrel lock.
8. Thread cable through housing.
9. Fasten cable to bolt on brake body. Use second hand to hold brake shoes firmly pressed against rim.
10. Tighten cable bolt.
11. Turn adjustable barrel to tighten brake cable (if necessary).

Tightening Loose Brake Levers

Loose brake levers should rarely be a problem on the road. Because your hands are often in contact with them, you will know immediately if a brake lever is loose—if it gives in your grasp as you apply pressure to it (the kind of pressure you apply when you get out of the saddle). If you feel looseness in a brake lever as you leave home, stop and tighten it before riding any farther.

A taut, tightened brake lever is more than just a well-maintained piece of equipment—it's a matter of safety. Cyclists use brake levers to rest their hands, particularly when getting out of the saddle. A loose brake lever is like a loose steering wheel on a car; imagine driving your car with a loose steering wheel.

Occasionally, the brake levers will appear tight as you roll away from home, only to loosen some miles down the road. Here, the usual culprits are vibration and stress.

If this happens to you, stop immediately. Take out the three-way wrench (for some brands, the set of allen keys is necessary) from your tool bag. Loosen the brake cable at the bolt that holds the cable to the brake body. You must loosen the brake cable, because the bolt that holds the brake lever to the handlebars sits immediately behind the brake cable. In order to get to the brake-lever bolt and tighten it, you'll have to slacken the brake cable to get it out of the way.

With the brake cable loosened, open the brake lever (which should now open without resistance). Grab the brake cable and pull it to the side far enough to gain unimpeded access to the bolt holding the brake lever to the handlebars.

Before you tighten the brake lever, straddle the bicycle to make sure the brake lever is facing straight ahead. If it's cocked slightly to the side, give it a firm tap with the palm of your hand. Occasionally, you will find that you can't budge the brake lever even though it is loose. If this is the case, loosen the bolt holding the brake lever to the handlebars and straighten the brake lever before tightening the bolt.

To tighten the bolt holding the brake lever to the handlebars, you will probably need an eight- or ten-millimeter socket wrench. This you have in the form of your three-way wrench. But you will discover that the three-way wrench is not the perfect tool for this adjustment. The fact is, the three-way wrench is a little short to get the job done easily. But the three-way wrench *will* tighten the bolt—just not as easily as the specialized wrench specifically designed for this repair. (I don't recommend bringing the specialized wrench along on the road, because it's fairly bulky and is not often needed.)

With some brakes, you will need an allen wrench to tighten the bolt holding the brake lever to the handlebars. At first this might seem easier than struggling with the three-way wrench. But you'll have to insert the long end of the allen wrench into the bolt, leaving you with the quarter-inch short end of the L-shape to get the task accomplished. This provides you with little leverage to tighten the bolt.

Once the bolt holding the brake levers to the handlebars is tightened, you need to refasten the brake cable to the brake body, according to the steps outlined on page 36.

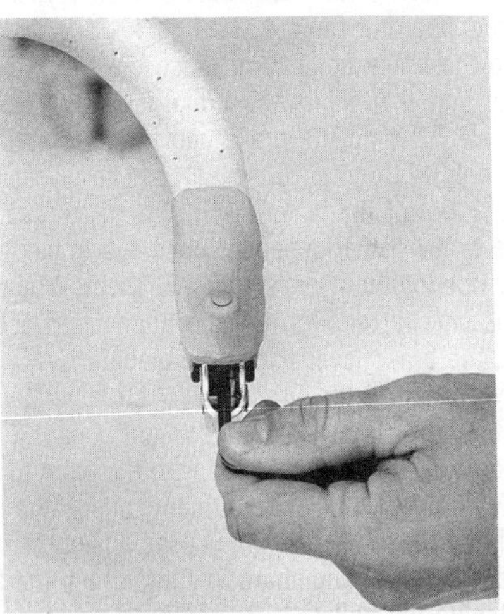

Tightening the brake lever using an allen wrench.

SUMMARY ON TIGHTENING BRAKE LEVERS

1. *At home:* Check looseness in brake levers as you begin to ride. If loose, return home to tighten.
1. *On the road:* Remove three-way wrench from tool-kit bag.
2. Loosen bolt holding brake cable to brake body.
3. Open brake lever widely.
4. Pull brake cable aside to gain access to bolt holding brake lever to handlebars.
5. Straddle bicycle to check that brake lever is facing straight ahead. If not, straighten by tapping with palm.
6. Tighten brake-lever bolt holding lever to handlebars (using the three-way wrench or an allen key, depending on the kind of brakes you have).
7. Fasten brake cable to brake body.

DERAILLEUR ADJUSTMENTS

Adjusting the Rear Derailleur

One of the most irritating problems in cycling occurs when you pull back on your rear derailleur lever and watch helplessly as your chain skids off the freewheel into that nether zone between the freewheel and the wheel itself. You have no choice but to stop and place the grimy chain back on the freewheel by hand.

Yet if the derailleur is adjusted properly, the chain won't slip off the freewheel. Fortunately, derailleur adjustment is a simple process. It must be done periodically, as the stresses and vibrations of riding act to throw the rear derailleur out of adjustment over time. If, in shifting to the lowest or highest sprocket on the freewheel, the chain does come off, stop immediately before the chain becomes lodged in between the wheel and the freewheel so securely that it cannot be pulled out.

How does the rear derailleur work? It consists of a rectangular boxlike body that swings in and out. The chain is wrapped

A poorly adjusted rear derailleur could result in the chain's lodging itself in the gap between the freewheel and the spokes.

around two rollers connected to the derailleur body. As you pull back or push forward on the derailleur lever, you increase or lessen the tension on the derailleur cable, forcing the derailleur body to swing in or out, and push the moving chain from one cog on the freewheel to the next. Pull back hard, and the chain will skip several cogs all at once.

But there is a limit to the motion of the rear derailleur. At a certain point, the derailleur will stop swinging. If properly adjusted, the derailleur will stop swinging on the innermost and outermost cogs of the freewheel.

If your derailleur pushes the chain so far that it falls off the freewheel, or if it doesn't push the chain far enough to get it onto the largest or the smallest cog, it is not properly adjusted.

The devices that limit and regulate the motion, or ''travel,'' of the derailleur are the stop screws. To find the stop screws on your rear derailleur, push the derailleur lever forward as far as it will go. Now pick up the rear wheel and, with your free hand, turn the pedal a few times until the chain has shifted all the way (the derailleur pushes the chain from cog to cog only when the chain is moving). Now look closely at the rear derailleur. You should find the rear derailleur body resting (or stopped)

The stop screws limit the travel of the rear derailleur when they sit squarely against the derailleur body.

against a small screw. This is the stop screw that limits the outer travel of the rear derailleur.

Now pull the derailleur lever back as far as it will go, again lifting the rear wheel and turning the pedal a few times to allow the chain to shift. Again look carefully at the rear derailleur and you will see the rear derailleur body resting against a second small screw. This is the stop screw that limits the *inner* travel of the rear derailleur.

The rear derailleur has two stop screws, to limit the rear derailleur's travel in either direction.

If you tried the above exercises and the chain shifted smoothly to both the smallest cog and the largest cog, then you have a correctly adjusted rear derailleur. If the chain fell off the freewheel or failed to reach the inner- or outermost cogs, then you need to adjust the stop screws on your rear derailleur.

If the rear derailleur didn't swing far enough to allow the chain to shift onto the outer or inner cogs, do the following:

1. If the chain will not go onto the smallest cog, push forward on the derailleur lever as far as it will go. If the chain will not go onto the largest cog, pull back on the derailleur lever as far as it will go. Now get out the flat-blade or Phillips screwdriver or the set of allen keys (depending on the kind of stop screws your derailleur has). Insert the screwdriver or allen key into the head of the stop screw. Turn the screw so that it backs away from the derailleur body, thus increasing the travel of the derailleur. If you're adjusting the *outside* travel, then increasing the travel of the stop screw will allow the derailleur to swing farther out. If you're increasing the *inside* travel of the derailleur, increasing the travel will allow the derailleur to swing in.

Be careful, though. Don't start turning like a carpenter fastening rivets. You need the precision of a watchmaker and the caution of a banker. Try turning the stop screw just a quarter turn. Then get on the bike and and try shifting to that last cog by pulling back on the derailleur lever (if you're shifting to the inside, largest cog) or by pushing forward on the derailleur lever (if you're shifting to the outside, smallest cog). If you hear a grinding sound and see the chain trying but failing to reach the final cog, then you need to open the stop screw a little more. Keep turning the stop screw and testing the results until you are able to shift onto the final cog without any difficulty. *Caution:* Be careful not to open the stop screw too far—you may find the chain shifting off the freewheel.

2. If your derailleur travels too far and the chain jumps off the freewheel, the first step is to free the chain and place it back on the closest freewheel cog. (Unless you brought a rag or some paper towels, your hands are bound to become greasy.)

Here again you will need a flat-head screwdriver, Phillips-head screwdriver, or an allen key to make the adjustment. The object is to adjust the rear-derailleur stop screws so that there is less travel. This will limit the movement of the derailleur so that the chain will no longer be thrown off the freewheel, but not limit it so much that the chain will no longer reach the inner or outer cog of the freewheel.

As in the opposite case, this is a trial-and-error process. But it is better in this case to overcompensate—to tighten the screws too much at first. If you close the stop screws too much, the worst that will happen is that the rear derailleur won't reach the inner or outer cog (you can then fine tune the stop screws to correct for that). But if you don't close the stop screws enough, the chain will once again jump off the freewheel—a frustrating setback.

When both stop screws are properly adjusted, the chain should travel all the way to the innermost, largest cog (when you pull back on the derailleur lever) and all the way to the outermost, smallest cog (when you push forward on the derailleur lever) smoothly and without threat of jumping off the freewheel.

When the stop screws are correctly aligned, the chain should travel to the innermost (shown here) and outermost cogs on the freewheel. No more, no less.

SUMMARY ON ADJUSTING THE REAR DERAILLEUR

1. Remove flat-blade or Phillips-head screwdriver or allen key (depending on derailleur brand) from your tool kit.
2. Place the screwdriver or allen key in the appropriate stop screw and turn to adjust derailleur travel. (If the chain has been thrown off the freewheel, turn the stop screw to limit travel. If the chain won't reach the inner or outer cog, open the stop screw slightly to extend travel.)
3a. If derailleur throws the chain off the freewheel, it is better to overcompensate on adjustment.
3b. If derailleur doesn't travel far enough (for the chain to reach inner or outer cog), it is better to underestimate and adjust in small increments.

Adjusting the Front Derailleur

Like the rear derailleur, the front derailleur occasionally falls out of adjustment. When it does, the derailleur will either not quite manage to shift the chain from chainring to chainring, or it will throw the chain off the chainwheel entirely.

Although the crescent-shaped front derailleur looks quite different from the rear derailleur, it is adjusted exactly the same way. The front derailleur quite literally pushes the chain from chainring to chainring. Like the rear derailleur, it is controlled by a cable attached to the derailleur lever. When you pull back on the lever, the derailleur pushes the chain onto the larger chainring; when you push forward, the derailleur forces the chain onto the smaller chainring. As with the rear derailleur, the action of the front derailleur is regulated by a pair of stop screws.

If the chain won't reach the big, outer chainring (it should *always* reach the inside chainring), or if it throws the chain too far, pushing it beyond the chainring, then your front derailleur needs to be adjusted.

The front derailleur is a much simpler mechanism than the rear derailleur. A pair of stop screws determines the front derailleur's travel.

The first step is to replace the chain on the chainring (if it has fallen off the chainring entirely). For ease of placement, I recommend pushing the derailleur lever forward (thus setting the front derailleur for the inner, small chainring) and placing the chain onto the small chainring. The reason for this is that the smaller size of the inner chainring exerts less tension on the chain (and less tension makes the chain easier to handle).

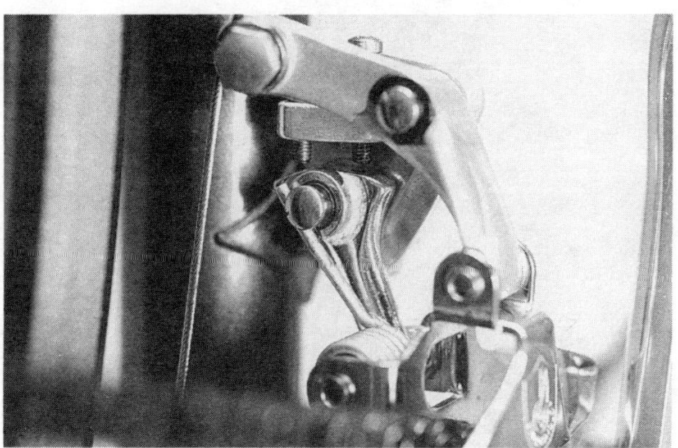

A close-up of the front-derailleur stop screws.

Next, get out the flat-blade or Phillips-head screwdriver or allen key (depending on the kind of derailleur you have) from the tool bag and locate the stop screws. On the vast majority of front derailleurs, these are found near the bolt that secures the derailleur cable to the front derailleur. On some models, the stop screws sit side by side; on others, they are farther apart. With most front derailleurs, the inside stop screw limits the inside travel and the outside stop screw limits the outer travel. But the only way to know for sure which stop screw controls each motion is to pull back on the derailleur lever and look closely to see which stop screw is riding against the derailleur body and limiting its motion. Now push the lever forward and see which stop screw limits the motion in that direction.

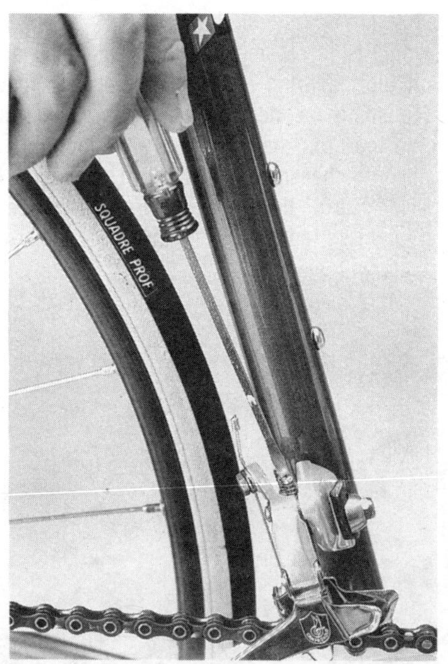

The stop screws are adjusted by means of a screwdriver.

If your front derailleur swings too far out, throwing the chain off the chainring (usually this happens only with the outer chainring), then you need to limit the front derailleur's travel. Turn the stop screw so that the derailleur body moves inward. If you turn the stop screw and the front derailleur begins to shift outward, you know you're turning in the wrong direction. For this problem, it's better to initially overadjust by turning the stop screw a couple of full turns. If you overadjust, the chain may no longer reach the outer chainring. Then it's just a matter of readjusting by turning the stop screw in small increments in the opposite direction and testing. If you don't adjust the stop screw enough initially, your chain will be thrown off the chainring again when you test it.

If, when shifting, your derailleur cannot reach the outer chainring, then you need to extend the travel of the front derailleur. In other words, the front derailleur won't reach the outer chainring because it isn't swinging out far enough. To extend the travel of the front derailleur, locate the stop screw that controls the outside travel of the front derailleur.

In making this adjustment, turn the stop screw a little bit at a time and test the derailleur motion. If you turn it too much, you'll overextend the adjustment and the chain will be thrown off the chainring.

Here is a chain that has been thrown off the chainring by a maladjusted front derailleur.

In my experience, the front derailleur falls out of adjustment much less frequently than the rear derailleur. This is true because there is much less stress on the front derailleur; with the rear derailleur, the chain is wrapped around the derailleur rollers, exerting constant tension on them. You also shift much more frequently with the rear derailleur, because there are more gears in the back to shift.

SUMMARY ON ADJUSTING
THE FRONT DERAILLEUR

1. Remove flat-blade or Phillips-head screwdriver or allen key (depending on derailleur model) from tool-kit bag.
2. Place screwdriver or allen key in stop screw and turn stop screw to adjust derailleur travel. (If the chain has been thrown off the freewheel, turn the stop screw to limit travel. If chain won't reach inner or outer cog, turn stop screw to extend travel.)
3. If derailleur is throwing the chain off the chainring, it is safer to overcompensate on adjustment and then fine tune. However, if the derailleur doesn't travel far enough to push the chain onto the chainring, adjust cautiously and check the results until the adjustment is correct.

Dealing with a Loose Front-Derailleur Clamp

One rare but not unheard-of front-derailleur ill is a shifting of the entire unit from its place on the bicycle frame, which causes a buckling effect that renders the derailleur useless. If you have a bicycle that has a brazed-on front derailleur (in which the front derailleur is not clamped to the frame but attached to a bolt that is a piece of the frame), this shifting is physically impossible.

But in the vast majority of cases, the front derailleur is attached to the frame by means of a clamp. This ringlike clamp fits snugly around the down tube of the frame (the tube that runs from the seat and seat post to the bottom bracket). It is fastened on the left side (viewed from behind) of the bike by a bolt. If the front derailleur is properly secured, the unit should never come out of adjustment. In fact, front-derailleur clamps can loosen over time due to poor workmanship, road stress, vibrations, and accidents.

If the front-derailleur clamp does come loose, stop immediately. You will know the clamp is loose if the derailleur begins to slide down the down tube or moves sideways. If you notice one of these symptoms, check the clamp by hand; if you feel any give whatsoever, your clamp is loose.

A loose front derailleur will not only preclude you from using the front derailleur, but it will probably also impede the chain from running smoothly across the chainrings.

Remove the three-way wrench (or allen wrench for some brands) from your tool bag. Because the derailleur cable puts downward tension on the derailleur, you will first need to remove the derailleur cable from the front derailleur. To do so, unfasten the bolt on the front derailleur that secures the derailleur cable. Now the front derailleur should be loose and free, and it will be much easier to properly position it without struggling to hold it up against the tension of the derailleur cable.

Now the question is, how do you position the front derailleur properly? And there is no exact answer. There are, however, a few guidelines. Looking at the derailleur from the side, you must position the bottom of the front derailleur body (the crescent shape) about an eighth of an inch above the sprockets of the chainring. When you do this, you'll find in the vast majority of cases that the curvature of the front derailleur body is approximately the same as that of the big chainring.

Look at the front derailleur from directly above. You'll see the two sides of the front derailleur, which will look like a box surrounding the chain. Place the front derailleur so that the sides of the box are more or less parallel with the chain. Now tighten the bolt and refasten the derailleur cable.

With some front-derailleur brands, you may notice that when

one side of the box is parallel with the chain, the other side of the box isn't parallel. If this is the case, you'll have to play around with the positioning of the derailleur until it works for your bike.

The reason your front derailleur's "box" doesn't have parallel sides is usually to allow for a wide variety of freewheel-chainwheel combinations. Here is how to test the position of this kind of front derailleur: Place the chain on the innermost, biggest cog of the freewheel and on the outermost, largest chainring in front. Tighten the bolt holding the front derailleur to the frame, but not all the way (the derailleur should be tightly mounted, yet loose enough so that it can turn slightly when you push it hard). Although you shouldn't use this combination in your riding (because it stretches out the chain and wears out both derailleurs), this is a "crossover" limit position for the chain that will test if your front derailleur is correctly adjusted. Turn the chain a few times (by pedaling or grabbing the pedal with a hand and raising the rear wheel a few inches off the ground). If you hear or see the chain rubbing against the front derailleur, push the front-derailleur body very slightly until you hear no more rubbing, but don't go beyond that point. Tighten the bolt that holds the front-derailleur clamp to the frame.

Now put the chain in the opposite diagonal combination, so that it's on the outermost small cog of the freewheel in the rear and the inner, small chainring in front. Again, turn the chain a few times and listen for the chain rubbing against the front derailleur. If you hear no rubbing, the position on the front derailleur is correct. Tighten the bolt that holds the front derailleur to the frame and continue with your ride.

If you do hear rubbing, loosen the bolt holding the front derailleur to the frame slightly and, while looking from directly above, ever so slightly turn the front-derailleur body. Turn the chain again. If you hear rubbing, continue to adjust the front derailleur body, again slightly. Continue until the rubbing noise stops.

Now you must apply the litmus test of front-derailleur adjustment. Put the chain back on the innermost, big cog of the freewheel and the outer, large chainring. Turn the chain. If you hear no rubbing, you have at last succeeded. Tighten the bolt that holds the front derailleur to the frame and continue riding.

But if you continue to hear rubbing, you have a ''rubber,'' a front derailleur that cannot be adjusted without rubbing in either one of the limit positions of the chain. My advice in this case is to live with it. You should never use these limit chain positions with such excessive crossover anyway, and you shouldn't hear any rubbing in any other freewheel-chainring combinations. In this case, your front derailleur is as well adjusted as it can be.

SUMMARY ON DEALING WITH A LOOSE FRONT-DERAILLEUR CLAMP

1. Remove the three-way wrench from tool-kit bag.
2. Loosen the derailleur cable from front-derailleur body.
3. Place bottom of front derailleur arm an eighth of an inch from top of sprockets of big chainring.
4. Turn front-derailleur body so that it is parallel with chain running through its ''box.''
5. If front-derailleur ''box'' isn't parallel with the chain, place the chain in its ''crossover'' limit positions (inside freewheel cog and outside chainring or outside freewheel cog and inside chainring). Adjust front-derailleur body until you hear no more rubbing.
6. Tighten bolt holding front derailleur to frame.
7. Tighten bolt holding derailleur cable to front derailleur.

ADJUSTING YOUR SEAT POST

Adjusting the seat post is something you shouldn't have to do very often. The seat post is the metallic tube that sticks out of the frame and attaches under the seat. The height of the seat post should be determined in an exact, rigorous manner when calculating your position on the bike. A lot of people think that specific seat position on the bike is a bunch of hogwash, but they're wrong. As a matter of fact, correct position on the bike is the single most important factor in determining how any given bike will function for you.

Getting the right size in running shoes or ski boots is important. Cycling is no different; the bike is an extension of your body. It's a little like marriage: if you aren't compatible, it isn't going to work out. For a detailed discussion of it, I recommend getting a copy of my book *Greg LeMond's Complete Book of Bicycling* and then having a bike-store professional measure your exact fit with the Fit Kit device.

Perhaps most surprising to cyclists not well-versed in the science of fitting is the number of different adjustments that have to be made. Most people think of fit as simply the height of their bicycle and a subsequent seat-post adjustment.

But that's only the first element. The horizontal length of the bike is equally important, as are the width of the handlebars, the length of the crankarms, and the position of the cleats on your shoes.

Fit is a lengthy and complex topic that deserves a substantive discussion. But a few basics about adjusting your seat post are in order here:

1. Measure your inseam by standing on a level, hard surface wearing thin socks and no shoes. Take a thick book and put it in your crotch as if it were your cycling saddle. Mark the top of the book with a pencil on the wall. That measurement is your inseam.

2. Frame size is determined by taking the inseam measurement you took and multiplying it by .65. For example, if your inseam is 30 inches, or 76.2 centimeters, your frame size should

be 19.5 inches, or 49.5 centimeters. *Caution:* This is a generalized formula. If you have an exceptionally long torso or exceptionally long legs in relation to your overall height, you may need to fit your bike accordingly.

3. After selecting a frame size, you need to adjust the seat post to determine your overall height on the bike—that is, the distance from the bottom bracket axle to the top of the saddle. This figure is arrived at by taking the measurement for your inseam and multiplying it by .88. In the above example, in which the inseam measure was 30 inches, overall height would now be 26.5 inches, or 67.3 centimeters. *Caution:* This measurement describes the distance from the center of the bottom bracket axle to the top of the saddle (the cupped portion in which you sit).

Once you've determined the right seat-post adjustment, you shouldn't fool around with it. Poor seat-post adjustment results in bad position, which will be detrimental to your cycling and may even lead to injuries, just as ill-fitting boots can. Though seat posts rarely fall out of adjustment, this can happen when you transport your bike, for instance, and find you have to remove the seat post for one reason or another. Unless you mark the height in some way, you'll have only an approximate idea of where it was before.

The remedy in this case is simple. Wrap tape (not Scotch tape, but bicycle-handlebar tape, electrician's tape, or masking tape) a couple of times at the exact point where the seat post ends, next to the top of the frame. This way, when you remove the seat post, you'll put it back in place at the same spot.

If you notice that your seat post is slipping down, the only plausible cause is a loose seat-post bolt. This is an exceedingly rare occurrence. In fifteen years of riding, it has never happened to me yet. And because it is rare, you need to view this incident with a healthy dose of suspicion if it happens to you. Most likely you have a stripped seat-post bolt.

To test this theory, take out the set of allen keys (or on some inexpensive models, a twelve-millimeter or American-standard socket wrench). First, pull up on the seat post until it's in the

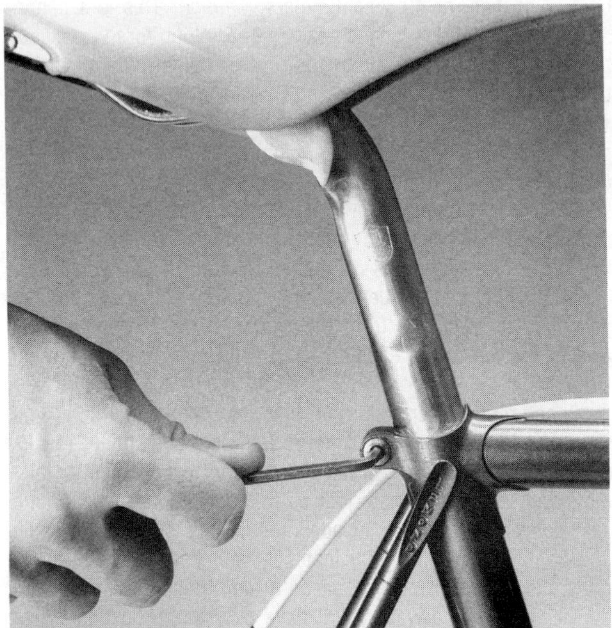

Tightening the seat-post bolt. Proper seat-post adjustment is crucial to cycling enjoyment. But if your seat post comes loose on the road, check to make sure the bolt isn't stripped.

right position. Next, tighten the seat-post bolt. If you feel it turn, at first easily, then harder, and then easily again, repeatedly, without tightening, you have a stripped seat-post bolt. Now it's time to make an emergency call. You can ride to the closest phone. If the bolt is very loose, you won't be able to sit on the seat, and riding standing up is fatiguing.

If, on the other hand, the seat-post bolt tightens after a few turns of the allen key, your seat post is fine. But you should ask yourself why the seat-post bolt was loose. Did you recently remove the seat post and seat and fail to tighten it sufficiently when you reassembled it? Did somebody else take it apart (for example, a mechanic) and fail to tighten it?

SUMMARY ON ADJUSTING YOUR SEAT POST

1. *At home:* Tape bottom of seat post to mark exact position.
2. Remove allen key from tool-kit bag.
3. Place seat post at correct position (determined by tape).
4. Tighten seat-post bolt.
4a. If seat-post bolt is stripped, call home.
4b. If seat-post bolt is not stripped, search for reasons why it came loose.

Adjusting the Fore and Aft Position of the Seat

The seat, or saddle, is attached to the seat post by two rails that run underneath the seat. These rails fit into the top of the seat post, on which a bolt or number of bolts are tightened. Occassionally, the seat starts to loosen, usually under the normal strain of everyday use.

The most important item to keep in mind while refastening the seat to the seat post is that this adjustment affects your position on the bike. The railing under the seat allows about two inches of travel, and once you've loosened the bolts on the seat post, you can move the seat front or back.

Your seat is positioned to allow for the ideal pedaling position and for the ideal fore-aft position on the bike. A detailed explanation of both these procedures is available in *Greg LeMond's Complete Book of Bicycling.*

If your seat comes loose, reposition it as closely as possible to its original position. Then tighten the bolt on the seat post that holds the seat attached.

On most modern seat posts, this bolt, accessible directly under the seat, is fastened with an allen key. Some seat posts have two bolts, others only one. Some older models require an ordinary monkey wrench. The old Campagnolo Nuovo Record seat post has the bolt positioned above the seat post and above the railings of the saddles. It is very difficult to reach and requires patience or a special tool manufactured by Campagnolo.

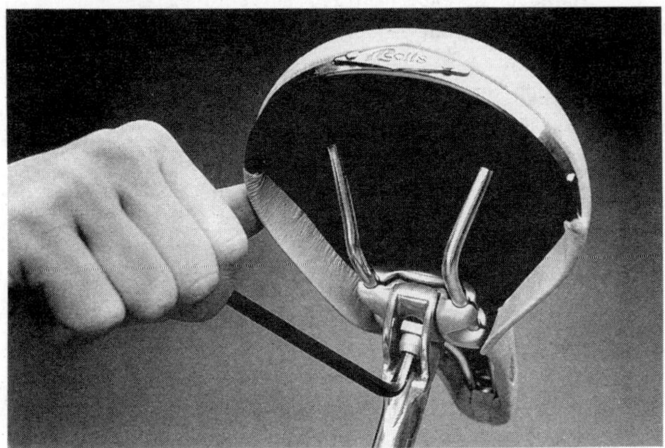

Adjusting the position of the seat.

ADJUSTING THE HANDLEBARS AND STEM

I don't think there's anything quite as annoying as riding with handlebars that aren't centered over the front wheel. This is a fairly common problem, especially after the handlebars and stem have been removed or reassembled, or after a crash.

If you find that your bars are off center, the problem is easy to remedy. Although it feels like the *bars* are off center, the problem actually resides in the handlebar *stem*. Take out the set of allen keys (on some inexpensive bikes, you need a twelve-millimeter or American-standard socket wrench). Loosen the bolt that holds the stem inside the frame.

Next, reposition your stem in the correct position by straddling the bike and looking down on the stem. Position the

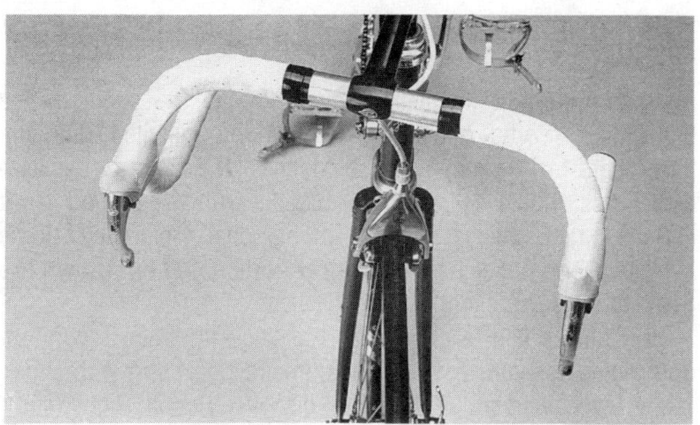

Riding with handlebars that are misaligned is both annoying and dangerous. To fix this problem, loosen the handlebar stem at the stem bolt (arrow) with a twelve-millimeter allen key.

handlebars as close to straight-ahead as you can and tighten the bolt holding the stem in the frame. But don't tighten all the way. You may discover upon second inspection that you've miscalculated and that the stem is still a little off center. Since you haven't entirely tightened the stem, nudge it gently with your hand until you're satisfied. Now finish tightening the bolt, holding the stem to the frame.

SUMMARY ON ADJUSTING THE HANDLEBARS AND STEM

1. Remove set of allen keys from tool-kit bag.
2. Loosen bolt holding stem to bicycle frame.
3. Straddle the bike and adjust the handlebars on straight-ahead center.
4. Tighten bolt holding stem to bicycle frame, but not all the way.
5. Double-check that handlebars are straight-ahead center.
6. Finish tightening bolt, holding stem to bicycle frame.

Adjusting the Handlebar Level

Another important handlebar adjustment is the angle of the handlebars. Some handlebars are poorly installed. For the handlebars to be properly installed, the flat portion at the handlebar tips should be practically parallel with the ground. To a certain extent, this is a matter of personal preference. Some cyclists prefer handlebars whose flat portions tilt up. Others like them to tilt down slightly.

But unless you're experienced at knowing what is comfortable riding for you, I would recommend beginning with a perfectly level position. If you later discover that a slight (and I emphasize slight) tilt is more comfortable, you can make that adjustment.

But if you tilt your bars way up before a long ride and discover that your hands keep slipping off the bars and that your arms are beginning to ache, you should reposition your bars.

To do so, take out the set of allen keys (on some bikes, you'll need the three-way wrench or even a twelve-millimeter or American-standard socket wrench). The bolt that secures the

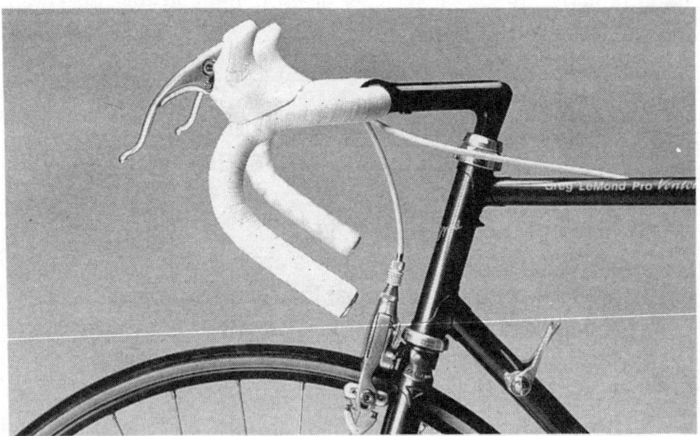

Poorly positioned handlebars. Notice that the bottom of the handlebars are at a steep angle. Although many cyclists ride with handlebars positioned like this, I find the position uncomfortable and even dangerous.

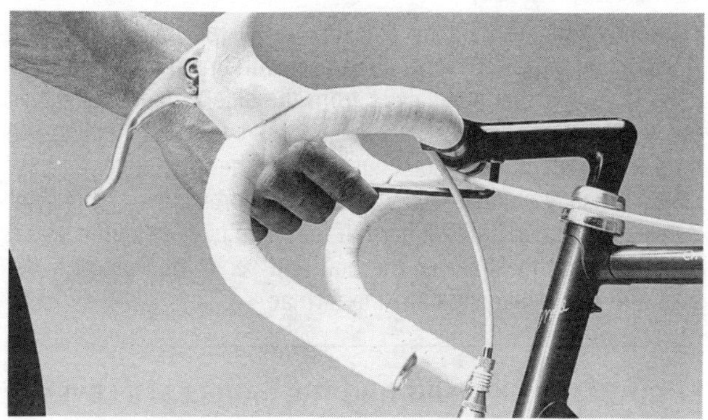

To reposition your handlebars, take a twelve-millimeter allen key (on most good bikes) and loosen the bolt binding the stem and handlebars.

Well-positioned handlebars with the drops practically parallel to the ground.

handlebars to the stem can be found on the stem, usually below and behind the spot where the bars enter the stem. To loosen this bolt, turn counterclockwise. Don't loosen the bolt all the way, because if you do, the bars will flop about uncontrollably. That looseness will make it hard for you to hold them in place and tighten the bolt in the stem at the same time. Instead, loosen the bolt just enough so that the bars can be turned in the grip of the stem.

Reposition the bars by placing the flat portion of the bars (the part near the tips) level or parallel with the ground (you may need to look at the handlebars from the side to make sure they are level). When you're satisfied, tighten the bolt holding the bars to the stem. This bolt must be fastened as tightly as possible. When you ride, you put a lot of pressure on the joint between the stem and the bars. If that joint is even a little loose, it could crack the bars or the bolt and send you flying off the bike and ignominiously onto the tarmac.

SUMMARY ON ADJUSTING THE HANDLEBAR LEVEL

1. Remove allen keys from tool-kit bag.
2. Loosen bolt holding handlebars to stem (but not all the way).
3. Looking at the handlebars from the side, position the flat portion of handlebars parallel with ground.
4. Retighten bolt holding handlebars to stem.

WHAT TO DO WHEN TOE CLIPS
BECOME LOOSE

Some of you may not have toe clips. Others may have the new strapless pedals (pioneered by the French manufacturer Look and imitated by a dozen others), which utilize a special cleat in your shoe to bind your shoe directly with the pedal.

But most cyclists still use toe clips (that metallic cage that fits around your shoe) and toe straps (the leather strap that tightens around your foot to hold it in place within the toe clips). This method of holding the foot secured to the pedals is an old feature of cycling, having first appeared before the turn of the century. It has changed little since then, and that fact is the source of its most common problems.

Toe clips are held in place by a couple of nuts and bolts, which occasionally come loose under the vibrations of riding.

The toe clip is never built onto the pedals. Instead, it is held there by a pair of nuts and bolts. Some pedals are designed to hold these nuts and bolts firmly in place and keep the toe clip from coming loose. But on many models, the inevitable road vibration and stresses can loosen the nuts and bolts over time. Usually you won't notice this until one of the bolts has fallen off the toe clip and is loose around your shoe. To avoid this, I suggest checking your toe clips before each ride.

If you're on the road and you feel your toe clips growing loose, stop and remove the three-way wrench from your tool bag. Most toe clips are secured with eight-millimeter nuts. Tighten them as much as you can. You may find, however, that without anchoring the bolt, the nut won't tighten, but instead will turn with the nut. Ideally, you should have an eight-millimeter socket wrench small enough to fit in the gap between the pedal body and the bolt. I didn't include this on the original list because the wrench takes up valuable space and is rarely needed. If your toe straps come loose chronically, I suggest you get a set of serrated washers that will keep the nuts firmly tightened (or, at worst, will allow you to tighten the nut without the second wrench in the unlikely event they do come loose again).

SUMMARY ON WHAT TO DO WHEN TOE CLIPS BECOME LOOSE

1. Remove three-way wrench from tool-kit bag.
2. Tighten nut holding toe clip to pedal.
3. If the toe clip slips with bolt, consider purchasing serrated washers for future use.

KEEPING YOUR WHEELS TRUE

The most delicate component on your bicycle is the wheel. Unlike the more solid parts on your bike, the wheel is made up of a strong but small hub and two thin strips of steel or aluminum called the rims. The glue that holds the wheel together is the spoke, a vermicelli-thin strip of steel that a child of five can easily bend in his or her hands. These spokes must shoulder your body weight *and* the stresses of riding.

Bicycle wheels have anywhere from twenty to forty spokes (thirty-two or thirty-six are most common). They are threaded together in careful combinations, each spoke crossing three or four others in most combinations. Take a look at your front wheel. Grab hold of any spoke where it intersects the rim. Slide your thumb and forefinger down until you come up to the intersection of the first spoke (this is usually halfway down the length of the spoke). That's one crossover. Keep sliding until you reach the hub. If your spoke intersects three spokes, then you know that every spoke on that wheel intersects three other spokes. This pattern of intersection gives the wheel its strength while allowing it to be remarkably light and flexible.

But, alas, the spokes *are* delicate. They fall out of adjustment and come loose very easily. This is especially true of the rear wheel, which bears much more stress. What happens to a wheel when spokes come loose is that it loses its true (the left-right alignment of the wheel). To test whether your wheels are true, take a direct overhead view at the point where the brake is positioned around the front wheel. Pick up the front wheel and spin it around a few times. Look carefully at the space between the brake shoes and the wheel. If the wheel runs through in a smooth motion, then you have a true wheel. If, on the other hand, you see that the wheel seems to waver to one side, or from side to side, then your wheel is out of true. Try the same thing with the rear wheel.

If the wheel is very much out of true, then it may rub against the brake shoes. You should always adjust your wheels at home before riding. You may need to take them to a professional if they are badly out of true.

If you're riding and you notice that a wheel is slightly out of true, you don't have to stop to retrue it—it's not an emergency problem. However, if the wheel starts to rub against the brake shoe, you should stop and remove the spoke wrench from the tool bag. Pick up the bike and spin the wheel in question slowly, until you spot the section of the wheel that is out of true.

To retrue the wheel, you must readjust spokes. But keep in mind that a wheel's true is a result of the combined tightness of all the spokes, not any single spoke. What that means is that if you tighten one spoke too much, you may ruin the balance among the other spokes. What is more, tightening one spoke too far could cause the wheel to lose its roundness (the circumference of the wheel as seen from the side).

Make sure that you're not tightening one spoke when its neighbor, which attaches to the opposite spoke at the center of the wheel, needs to be loosened. Beyond this, wheel trueing is a matter of feel and experience. Most likely, if you're on the road trying to quickly retrue a wheel, you'll be successful, even if you don't do a perfect job. And you can always take the wheel to a professional mechanic for a complete trueing job.

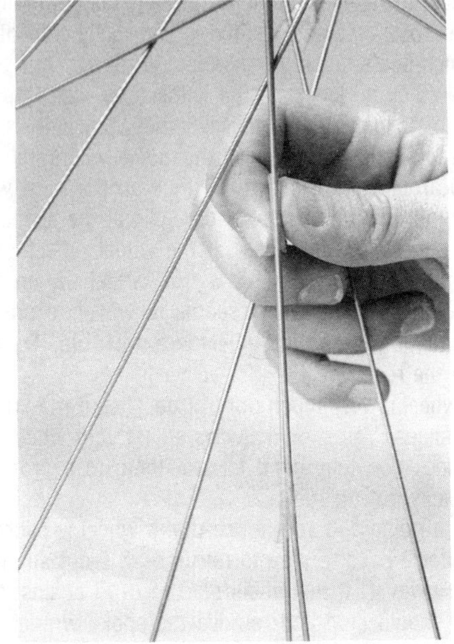

If you break a spoke, tape it to a neighboring spoke by using a piece of handlebar tape from your tool kit.

Another calamity that can befall wheels is a broken spoke. Since spokes are delicate, it is not uncommon for them to break. Luckily, most wheels are still ridable with one or two broken spokes. Think of a bicycle wheel with a broken spoke as the equivalent of the emergency minispare that automakers put in their cars.

If you do break a spoke, you will have to stop to remove or secure the broken spoke parts. Most spokes break somewhere near the hub, where the stress is greatest. If a front-wheel spoke breaks, first remove the front wheel from the bicycle frame. Then remove the lower portion of the severed spoke by threading it through its eyelet in the hub. To remove the top half of the severed spoke, which is still attached to the rim, you must remove the tire and inner tube or sew-up. Since that's impractical on the road, you can use the extra roll of bicycle-handlebar tape, which is standard issue in the Greg LeMond tool kit described above. Tape the broken spoke to its closest neighbor, so it won't get in the way of the other spokes. You'll be able to ride home safely, where you can replace the broken spoke at your leisure.

If you break a spoke on the rear wheel (which is far more likely), you may not be able to remove even the portion of the broken spoke attached to the hub if it's attached on the side next to the freewheel. In that case, tape both the lower and upper halves of the severed spokes to their neighbors. If the broken spoke is on the nonfreewheel side, you can operate as in the case of the front wheel.

SUMMARY ON KEEPING YOUR WHEELS TRUE

1. Remove spoke wrench from tool-kit bag.
2. Locate section of wheel out of true by turning wheel and watching the wheel's motion in relation to the brake shoes.
3. Tighten or loosen spokes to achieve trueness and roundness (spoke tension should be as equal as possible among all spokes).

CONCLUSION

The preceding text is intended to act as a guide in the case of emergency roadside repair. I have not covered every possible repair, nor have I covered every possible permutation of each repair. But I think you'll find that the basic explanations fit the majority of on-the-road breakdowns and will help you to get back on the road again.

Many of the ills described above can be avoided easily with good maintenance. Which brings me to the following section, devoted to that noble art.

2
BICYCLE MAINTENANCE

Like any machine, your bicycle will need to be maintained and repaired from time to time. Some maintenance should be done every few days, while other tasks can be done once a year. Fortunately, the bicycle is basically a simple machine and simple to keep up. Most cyclists can learn to do basic maintenance and repairs in a very short time. There are, however, certain repairs that require considerably more skill—some repairs should never be attempted by nonprofessionals.

Frankly, during the season, I rarely do my own repairs. Since I turned professional, and even before, I have always relied on the help of professional mechanics to keep up my bicycles. Of course, I do all my basic maintenance when I'm not around my team, in the winter, for example.

But I think the advice on maintenance should come from a true professional in the field. That's why I've asked professional mechanic Roland Della Santa to help me provide tips for this chapter. Roland was one of the first people to notice my riding. Later he became my first sponsor and built bikes for me. In 1985, Roland was the official Red Zinger team mechanic of the Coors Classic, which I won. He's a thoroughly professional designer, frame builder, and mechanic.

I will not tackle the advanced subjects of frame building, frame repair, and painting. These activities require special skills and tools. If you want to build your own bike, you will never learn enough about the field in a book—you should find a professional frame builder to study under. But be prepared to spend some time at it: It's a skill that takes years to acquire. Also, you'll have to spend a few thousand dollars purchasing equip-

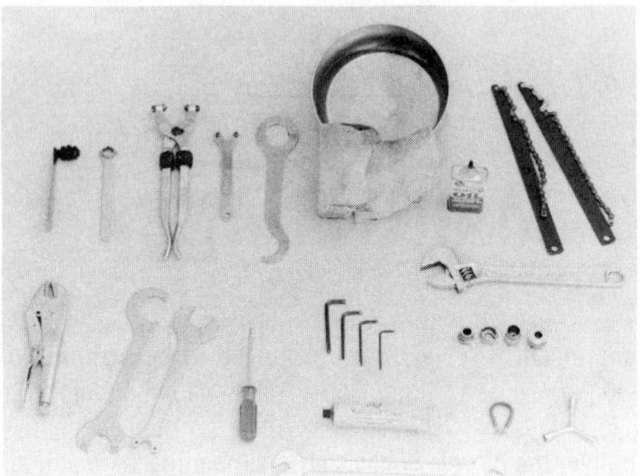

Starting with the right tools: A complete set of tools is the key to maintaining your bike. Tools (clockwise, starting in upper left-hand corner): crankarm remover, crankarm bolt remover, wire cutter, pin wrench, bottom bracket cup remover, container with wire basket for solvent, 3-in-One oil, two freewheel cog removers, adjustable wrench, various bolts, three-way wrench, spoke wrench, two-way wrench, tire glue, various allen-head keys, screwdriver, headset wrench, bottom bracket ring wrench, vise grip.

ment, and a few thousand more buying things like tubing, lugs, and soldering material.

If you're interested in repainting your frame, I recommend you go to a professional bike shop mechanic or frame builder who can give you a professional paint job for about fifty dollars. Some books outline a very complicated and drawn-out process for do-it-yourself painting. I just don't think it's worth it. You need specialized equipment. And chances are, unless you're already a professional, you'll end up with a less-than-professional paint job.

Frame repair may seem like the simplest of all the frame arts, but it's not. If you create a ''blip'' (as dents are known in cycling) in your frame, don't try to bang it out yourself. Take it to a professional bike shop or frame builder. Unless you are very careful, you could risk metal fatigue and a broken frame. Then you'll have to have your frame repaired by a professional at much higher cost. More probably, you'll have to buy an entirely new frame at yet higher cost.

Anybody who wants to maintain a bicycle needs to start out with the right tools. If you don't have the right tools, you're not going to be able to handle the simplest repair. Even if you don't plan on doing extensive work on your bike, you always need tools, even if it's only to tighten a screw or make an adjustment.

You must decide for yourself how many tools you want to own. But there are certain basic tools everybody should own.

The first tool you'll need is a bike stand. This will be the heart of your workshop. Although you can spend a lot of money on a bike stand, you can easily get away with a small stand that simply raises one wheel off the ground at a time. Such stands are cheap and light—they can even fit into a large tool box. Of course, if you want a stand that allows you to swing your bike as you work, you're looking at more money.

You will need a good set of wrenches that fit your bike. Most bikes have bolts in the eight- to twelve-millimeter range. There are many different kinds of wrenches. The most obvious is the monkey wrench. Monkey wrenches are usually the strongest and provide the most leverage. But if you need several different sizes, they can be unwieldy to use. In addition, you can't use an ordinary monkey wrench in certain tight spots.

If you want the strength of the monkey wrench but in a more practical form, get a socket wrench. You can usually find these at auto parts stores. They have one wrench arm and a wide range of sockets to fit it. The arm has a ratchet that makes it easy to change a bolt. You can also buy a combination wrench. These are usually much smaller and have three different bolt sizes, often eight, nine, and ten millimeters. This is a good wrench to have, especially on a ride, since you can just stuff it in your back pocket. A bicycle dumbbell wrench—an inexpensive combination wrench that fits eight different bolt sizes—is also useful, particularly on a long ride, on which you don't want to carry much weight.

If you have a recent-model bike you'll have a number of recessed-head or allen bolts. Most bikes have allen heads holding the chainrings to the crankarms, the stem in the frame, the derailleur to the dropout, and the seat post to the frame. Many Japanese bikes come with a couple of allen keys. But if you don't have them, buy a complete set of allen keys at a hardware store or bike shop: They're cheap and easy to use. If you have trouble holding on to your smaller allen wrenches, get a set held together by a large ring.

You'll need a special pedal wrench to take off your pedals. They usually come in thirteen- to sixteen-millimeter sizes. Most flat or cone wrenches will work here. Be careful, though, not to skimp on pedal wrenches. You can buy cheap ones that will bend if your pedals are very tight—and often pedals *do* get very tight—and ruin the pedal. Some pedals that use allen-head bolts don't require a pedal wrench. You can also use cone wrenches on most brake models. These narrow wrenches are used to straighten the brakes when they're rubbing on the wheels.

You will need a small cable cutter to install brake and derailleur cables.

Another important tool is the freewheel remover. Freewheel removers come in different shapes and sizes depending on the freewheel you have. Check with your dealer to determine which remover you need.

There are a number of smaller, inexpensive tools you'll need as well. A spoke wrench comes in handy to tighten spokes and straighten wheels at home when they get out of true. A chain tool is essential to remove the chain, something you'll need to do periodically. Depending on the kind of cranks you have, you may need a small, standardized crankbolt remover to remove the cranks when cleaning and regreasing the ball bearings. Many derailleurs use a small screwdriver to adjust their play.

You can get additional tools as you become more familiar with your bike. For example, unless you have a special sealed-bearing headset, you'll need to overhaul your headset every fifteen thousand miles or so. You could use a twelve-inch adjustable monkey wrench to undo the headset, but the adjustable wrench can easily slip and damage your headset. A specialized (and expensive) headset remover is better.

If you want to overhaul your bottom bracket (unless you have a sealed-bearing model), you'll need a specialized bottom bracket remover. This is usually a large tool that requires some experience to use. Similarly, if you want to *remove* your headset, you need a very large and expensive headset tool.

If you find yourself doing work that requires expensive tools, you can probably find a bike shop in your area that has loaner tools. These are tools that are set aside in an area of the bike shop for customer use. In most shops you pay to use them; in others they are free. In both cases you have to use them in the store.

One note of caution: If a repair becomes complicated and you start to become confused or frustrated, don't take it out on your bike. Guessing at how something works or forcing a bolt can damage your bike. Take the bike to a professional mechanic: it may cost you a little more money than if you had done it yourself, but it's a heck of a lot cheaper than buying a new bike.

Maintaining the Drivetrain

Let's start with the drivetrain. All the parts of your drivetrain should be well adjusted. Because of all the moving parts, the drivetrain will require your attention periodically.

Bottom Bracket

First, check the bottom bracket axle adjustment by taking off the crankarms with the crankarm remover. Loosen the bolt that holds the crankarm to the bottom bracket axle and remove the crankarms.

Next, turn the bottom bracket axle with your fingers. When perfectly adjusted it should turn smoothly with a few smooth ''bumps'' as it turns around. Next, grab the bottom bracket axle at both ends and pull back and forth. There should be no play whatsoever.

If the ''bumps'' feel rough, your bottom bracket is too tight. That can grind down the ball bearings. If, on the other hand, there is some play, the bottom bracket is too loose and you risk breaking the bottom bracket axle.

To readjust the bottom bracket axle, you'll need the special bottom bracket tool for your model. The cup that encloses the bottom bracket on the *chain side* is *not* adjustable. The other cup *is* adjustable, usually by means of a pin wrench that's specially designed for this purpose. To tighten, turn clockwise; to loosen, turn counterclockwise.

The bottom bracket should be adjusted exactly at the point at which there's no play, but before there's any roughness. Be careful, though, not to err on the side of looseness. If the axle has *any* play whatsoever, you can break the axle. After you find the exact point at which there is neither play nor looseness, give the pin wrench an extra turn of about five degrees (on a circular scale of 360 degrees).

Unless you have a sealed-bearing bottom bracket, you'll need to overhaul your bottom bracket every fifteen thousand miles or so. If you ride infrequently, the bottom bracket should be overhauled once a year.

To overhaul the bottom bracket, remove the chain so it doesn't get in your way. To remove the chain, take the chain tool, place it in any one of the links, tighten the tool and pop out the link. Next, remove the crankarms as described above, using the crankarm remover.

Once the crankarms are off, remove the adjustable cup on the side opposite the chain. Use the pin wrench and simply unscrew it slowly. With this adjustable cup off, the bottom bracket axle comes out easily. The axle can be cleaned by dipping it in some solvent, while the inside of the bottom bracket can be cleaned with a rag dipped in the same solvent. (Ordinarily, you don't need to remove the fixed cup. If you're changing bottom bracket assemblies, however, you will need to remove the fixed cup and install a new one. This requires a large, cumbersome tool called a fixed cup remover that takes a little training to master. Ask your local bike shop for assistance.)

When you remove the adjustable cup, you'll find that inside the cup is a set of ball bearings. Usually they come in a track called a *race.* On other models, the bearings are loose. Once your adjustable cup has been removed, tip the bike gently to the floor, with the open side of the bottom bracket toward the ground.

The axle should now come out. (In most cases, it'll have a plastic dust shield fitted around the center portion of the axle.) Next, tap the bike gently until the fixed cup ball bearings drop out.

You are now ready to clean the entire assembly with a powerful solvent. You can find a grease-cutting solvent in a bike shop or auto parts store. After cleaning the bearings, axle, and cup in the solvent, take all the parts and rinse thoroughly with water and dry them—if you don't rinse the bearings and the cup, the film of solvent on their surfaces will cut or dilute the new grease.

Now, take the ball bearings and dip them generously in a white lithium bicycle grease. You can find bicycle ball bearing grease at all bike shops. Be sure to coat the inside of the bottom bracket cups in grease, too. Be generous with the grease without being wasteful—use common sense.

Before you reinstall the parts, put some solvent on a rag and wipe out the inside of the bottom bracket itself. Use a medium-sized stick to get the rag all the way in. The threads on the inside of the bottom bracket where the adjustable cup screws on should also be cleaned. Take the rag in your fingers and wipe vigorously along the threads. Also wipe the threads on the adjustable cup.

To put the ball bearings that fit in the fixed cup back, place them around the axle, with the openings in the ball bearing race (if there is a race) facing out *toward* the fixed cup. Slowly move the axle through the bottom bracket. If your bike has loose bearings, you'll have to lay the bike on its side and fit the bearings into the fixed cup by hand. The bearings are held in place by additional grease in the cup.

Now, take the second set of ball bearings and place it in the adjustable cup. Carefully thread the cup back on the bottom bracket, making sure the ball bearings are still trapped between the axle and the adjustable cup. Once everything is back in place, tighten the adjustable cup as described above, until there is no play, but before you feel any roughness.

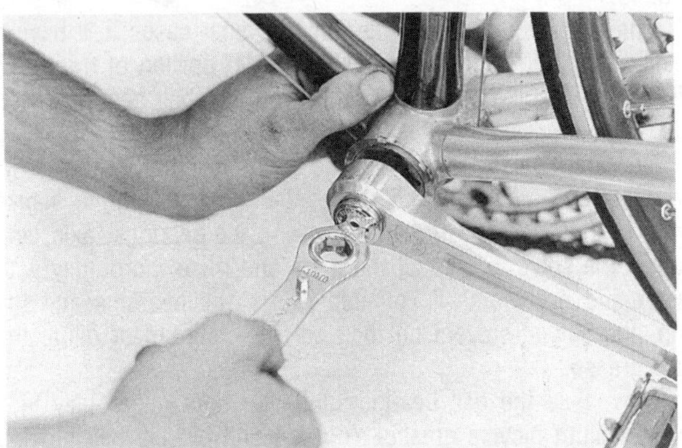

Removing crankarms. Remove dust cap (if you have one). Dust cap usually is removed with an eight-millimeter wrench.

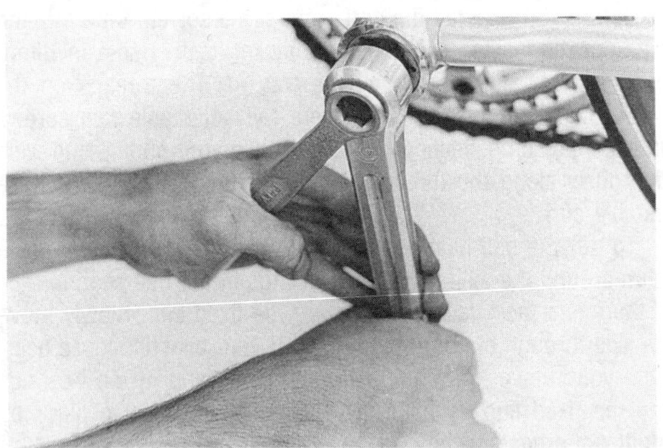

Remove the crankarm bolt with the special crankarm bolt remover.

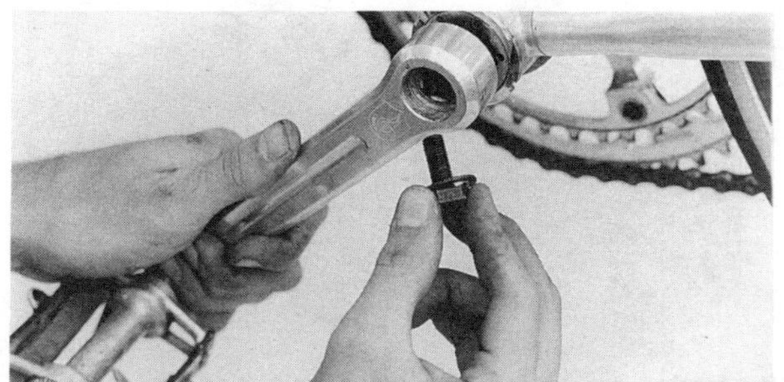

When crankarm bolt is removed, crankarms are still tightly in place.

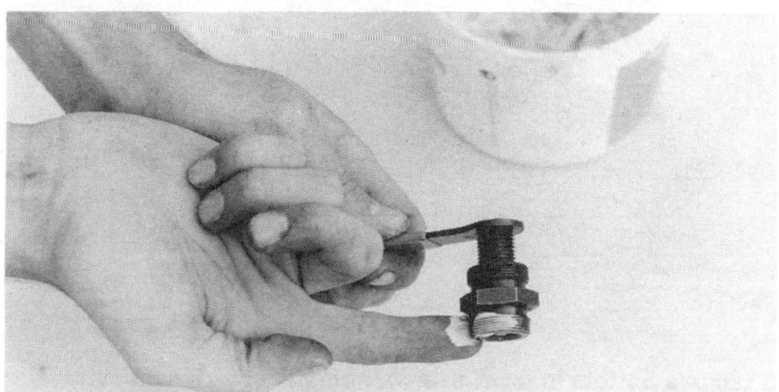

To remove crankarm, use crankarm remover. Grease end of crankarm remover before inserting.

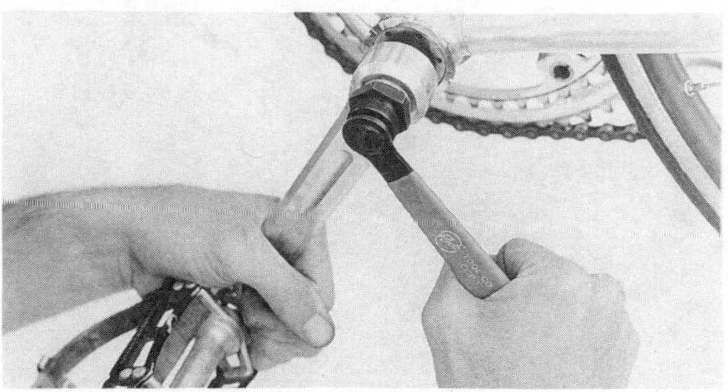

Insert crankarm remover slowly and turn.

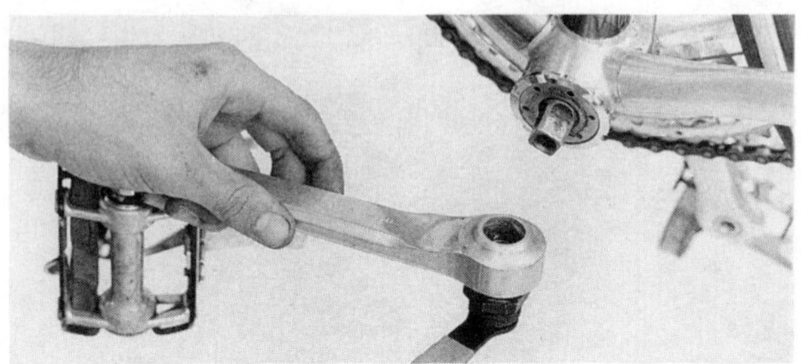

After turning, you will feel pressure. Keep turning until crankarm comes off bottom bracket axle. Then loosen gently to remove crankarm remover.

To remove bottom bracket axle, use ring wrench on *adjustable* cup ring (opposite the chain side). Loosen ring and remove.

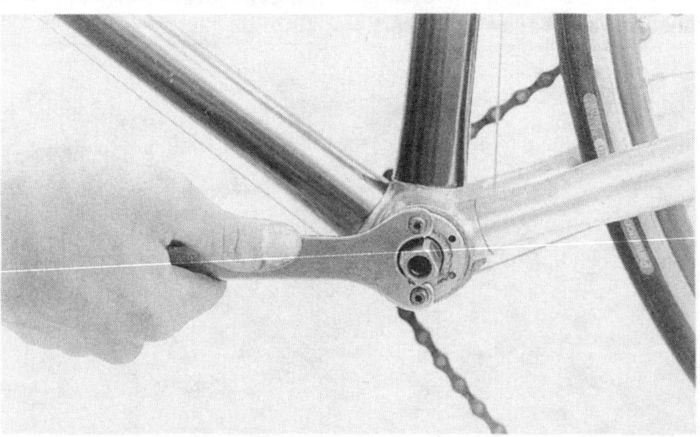

After ring is removed use *pin* wrench to remove adjustable cup.

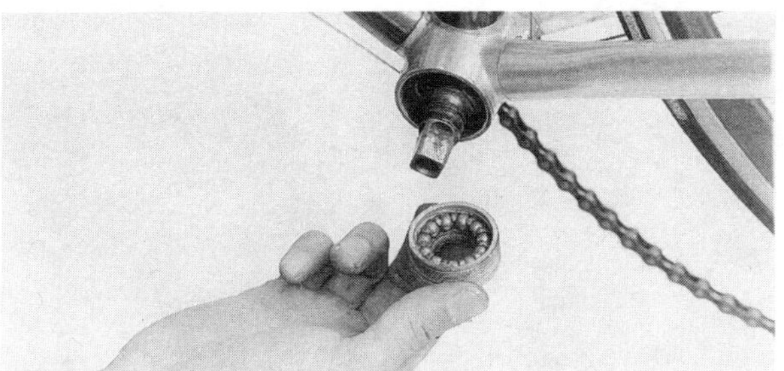

When adjustable cup is removed, you will notice a race of ball bearings on the inside.

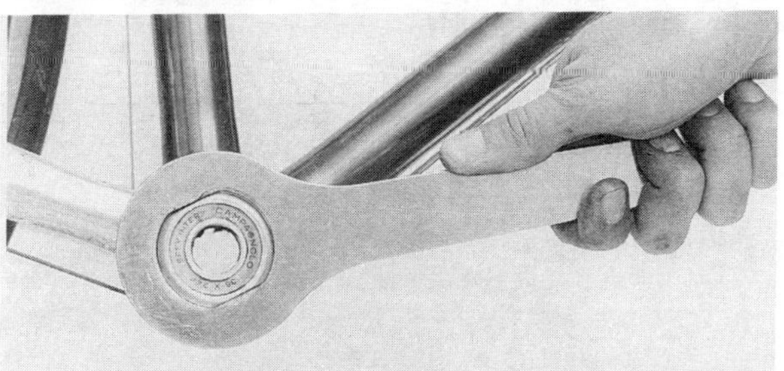

You may want to remove the *fixed* cup as well for a thorough overhaul, but this is not necessary. Note: You will need a special wrench to remove the fixed cup.

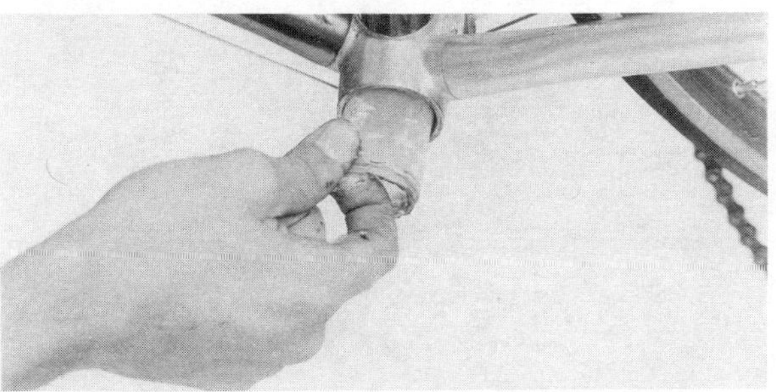

Most bottom brackets have a protective plastic dust shield. Remove and dip in solvent.

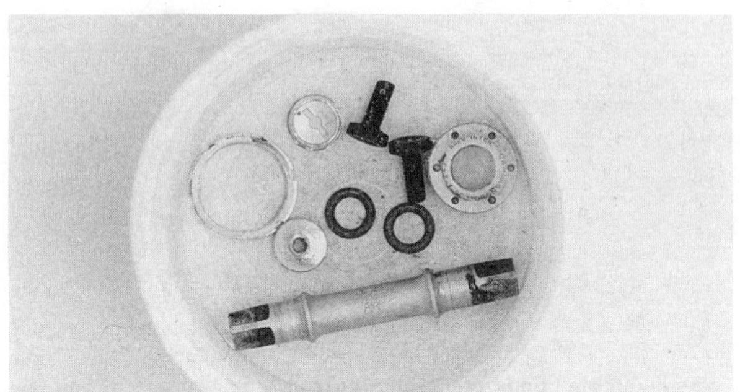

Place all bottom bracket parts in a bucket containing solvent. Clean and then rinse thoroughly.

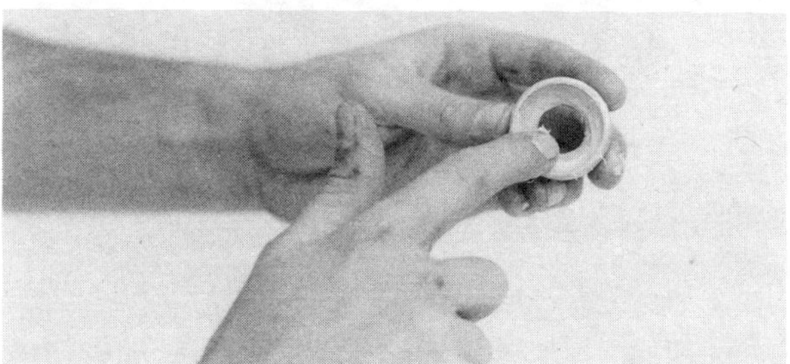

Carefully apply bicycle grease to the inside of the bottom bracket cups before reinstalling.

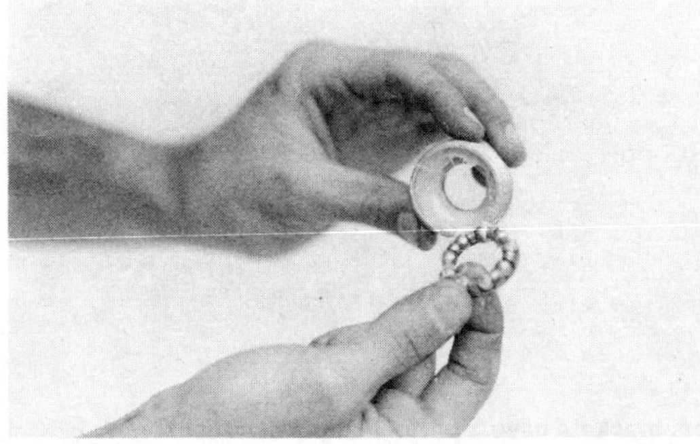

Lightly grease bearings and races and place inside cup.

Crankset

Your crankarms shouldn't require any special maintenance. Keep them clean with soapy water and a large, soft brush. Make sure to clean the dirt around the pedals, behind the spindle assembly, and down where the crankarm is attached to the bottom bracket.

Every seventy-five hundred miles or so, you should clean your crankset thoroughly. I recommend cleaning it in the same solvent you used on the bottom bracket. Ideally, you should take the chainrings off and clean all the nooks and crannies in the spindle assembly. You can clean the *teeth* in the chainrings with a *bristle* brush dipped in the solvent. (Make sure that you don't lose any of the allen bolts and nuts that hold the chainrings to the spindle assembly—put them in a small cup for safekeeping.)

When you put the chainrings back on, be sure to tighten the allen bolts progressively. Don't tighten one bolt all the way and then all the others afterward. Tighten each bolt until it starts to get a little tight. Then tighten all the bolts one by one.

Pedals

When you overhaul the crankset, you should also check the pedals. To remove the pedals, use a cone or flat wrench, or if you have it, an allen key on the recessed head at the end of the pedal spindle *behind* the crankarm.

Clean out the threads on the crankarm where the pedals are attached, as well as the threads on the pedal spindle.

You should overhaul your pedals every fifteen thousand miles. If you don't ride a lot, overhaul them at least once a year. If you ride in a lot of very bad weather you may have to perform maintenance on your pedals more frequently.

Most pedals on the market don't have sealed bearings. If yours do, they won't need any maintenance.

To overhaul pedals, remove them from the crankset as described above.

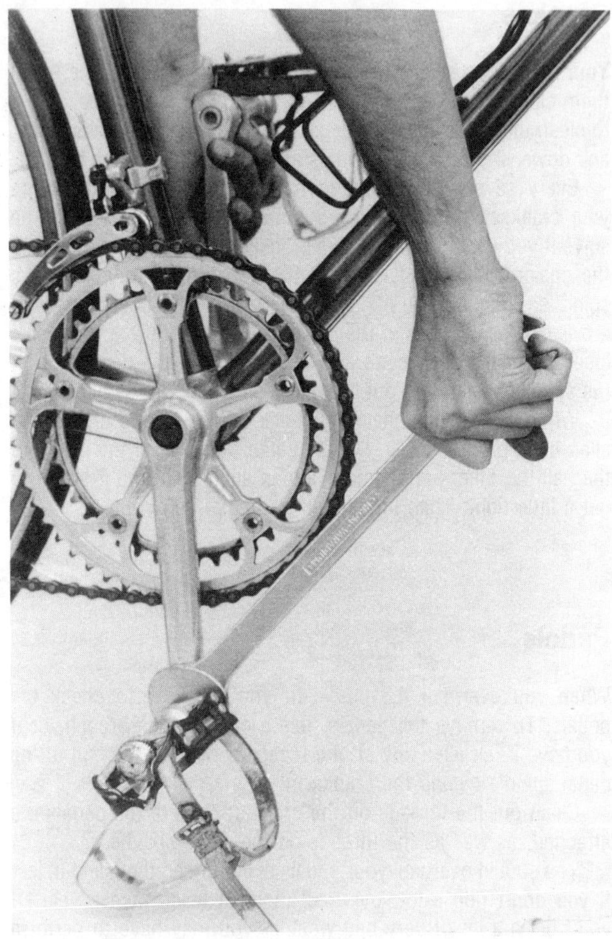

Removing pedals. Use a special flat wrench placed in the space between the crankarm and the pedal axle. Turn clockwise. Note how you need to grip the other crankarm solidly to keep the crankset from turning while you apply pressure.

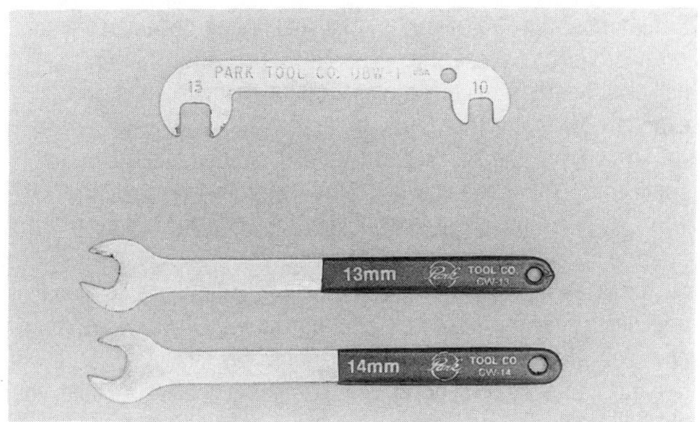

Different models of flat wrenches. These can be used on your pedals and brakes. Generally, pedal wrenches are longer to provide you with better leverage.

Once the pedals are off, the first step is to remove the dust cap on the outside of the pedal. You can do this with a small screwdriver—the dust cap should come off easily if it was correctly installed.

When you take off the dust cap, you'll notice a locknut. To remove this locknut, anchor the axle—either by gripping it in a vise or by holding a wrench to the ''flat'' next to the threads where the pedal is attached to the crankarms. With a vise, remember to always grip the pedal on the ''flat'' and never on the threads. The outside of the pedal should be facing up as you disassemble it.

Once the axle is anchored, take a small wrench or a special pedal locknut wrench and loosen the locknut. Remove the locknut and the locknut washer—you may need the help of a small screwdriver—and put both the locknut and its washer in a small cup.

With the locknut washer off, you'll be able to see the ball bearings. To remove them, grab a small cup or receptacle and slowly turn the pedal, letting the ball bearings fall into the cup. Be sure to hold on to the axle: you don't want to let it slip.

Sometimes, the ball bearings may stick in the pedal. Use a small screwdriver or tweezers to dislodge them. After this first set of ball bearings has been removed, count them, so that you know exactly how many there are.

To remove the second set of ball bearings, grab a second small cup. Tilt the pedal the other way and remove the axle. The ball bearings will follow. If any stick to the inside dislodge them with the screwdriver or tweezers.

Clean all parts with solvent. Use a bristle brush to clean off any heavy dirt. If your ball bearings are old and worn, buy a new set. If you get new ball bearings, always make sure you get the same size—a good way to assure that is to take your old ball bearings with you to the bike shop.

Once everything has been cleaned in the solvent and thoroughly rinsed, you're ready to reassemble your pedal. First, dip the ball bearing races (the tracks that hold the ball bearings together) in the white lithium grease. Also dip the pedal area that holds the ball bearings in grease. Use a generous amount of grease.

Take the ball bearings closest to the crankset and put them back in place. If you have bearing races this shouldn't be too hard and the grease will hold the race in place. If you have individual bearings, you'll need to tip the pedal so that the outside is slightly lower than the crankset side and put the ball bearings in one by one. The grease will hold them in place.

Once the crankset-side bearings are in place, insert the axle and push it all the way through. Then take the outside ball bearings and put them in place—that should be much easier to do than the first set of ball bearings.

Next, replace the locknut washer and thread the locknut by hand. When you can no longer turn it by hand, use a wrench to tighten it until there is no play, but before there is a roughness. A good rule of thumb is to tighten beyond the point at which you feel any play and then loosen an eighth of a turn. To finish the job thread the dust cap tightly by hand.

Front Derailleur

The front derailleur is a very simple component that usually requires little more than basic maintenance. The most common problem with a front derailleur is that the adjustment screws that control the travel of the derailleur from left to right are poorly set. If this happens, the chain can skip too far and fall off a chainring. If there's not enough travel the chain simply won't be able to change from one chainring to the next.

Because these screws can come out of adjustment under the stress of riding, it's always a good idea to be prepared to adjust your front derailleur, even when you're riding.

To adjust the screws on your front derailleur, you'll need a small screwdriver for most models (some derailleurs have small, ordinary allen-head bolts). On most models the screw closest to the frame adjusts the play of the front derailleur to the outside (the big chainring) and the screw on the outside adjusts the play to the inside. Double check on your front derailleur to see which screw adjusts which motion. You can do this by activating the gear lever back and forth and watching closely as the derailleur arm hits the screws.

Another common problem with the front derailleur is that the derailleur cable between the derailleur and the shift lever loses tension. If this happens, loosen the bolt that holds the cable—usually an eight-millimeter bolt—and pull the cable taut with your fingers. Then retighten the bolt. If this doesn't work, you'll need a pair of vise-grips; attach them to the end of the derailleur cable just beyond the front derailleur bolt and pull. Then tighten the bolt again. (Note: Be careful to wrap the end of the cable in a thick towel—otherwise the cable will become frayed and you may have to get another cable.)

If your front derailleur is poorly positioned on the frame (and doesn't reach the chainrings very well), you'll have to move it. On most models, a large clamp attaches the unit to the frame. Usually, the bolt that holds this clamp is on the nonchain side of the seat tube. Unfasten the clamp with an appropriate wrench. Sometimes, the front derailleur is attached with a brazed-on mount. In this case, you won't be able to adjust your front derailleur's position, but presumably the braze-on was installed in the factory in the right position.

Adjusting the front derailleur adjustment screw. Turning the stop screw limits the travel of the front derailleur. One screw limits inside travel, while the other limits outside travel. If your front derailleur is "throwing" the chain every time you shift, you need to adjust one of the adjustment screws.

To place your derailleur at the right spot on the frame, the bottom of the front derailleur cage should be about five millimeters from the top of the teeth on the large chainring. Make sure that the cage is straight, perfectly aligned with the chainrings when looking from above. Tighten the bolt on the clamp, and your front derailleur is installed.

If you change the size of your big chainring, you'll need to adjust the position of your front derailleur. This is only possible, of course, if you don't have the brazed-on derailleur mount. After you've installed your new chainring, simply follow the same procedure as above.

To clean your front derailleur, wash it in warm, soapy water every few hundred miles and scrub it with a large, soft brush.

Rear Derailleur

The rear derailleur is much more complicated than the front derailleur. It's composed of a parallelogram body that shifts to move the chain from sprocket to sprocket. It also has a set of rollers that maintain chain tension. The rear derailleur has about twenty moving parts.

As with the front derailleur, you have to make sure the adjustment screws are adjusted properly. If they aren't, your chain could skip beyond the freewheel sprockets if the adjustment allows the chain to travel too far, or it may restrict the chain from reaching the largest and smallest sprockets on either end if the adjustment doesn't allow the chain to travel far enough.

Use a small screwdriver or a conventional or allen-head wrench, depending on your model, to adjust the screws. Because models vary, you'll need to know which adjustment screw—top or bottom—adjusts the inside and outside movements of the derailleur. This is usually marked right on the derailleur, high or low (H or L).

If you find that your chain is going into your spokes, adjust the adjustment screw that limits the motion of the derailleur in that direction. Turn the screw a half turn and test your derailleur. If the chain still goes into the spokes, turn the adjusting screw

Adjusting the rear derailleur adjustment screws. The rear derailleur adjustment screws work the same way as those on the front derailleur, limiting inside and outside travel. After you adjust the screws, shift gears to check your adjustment.

another quarter turn. If the chain won't even reach the largest cog on the freewheel, on the other hand, then you've turned the adjusting screw too far. Turn it back in the other direction so that the chain skips easily onto the last cog without going into the spokes.

If the chain is skipping off the smallest cog (the one nearest to you as you face the bike) and into the gap between the freewheel and the frame stays, adjust the other screw on your derailleur in the same fashion.

When the adjusting screws on the derailleur are adjusted properly, the chain should skip freely to all the cogs and never off into the spokes or the gap between the freewheel and the frame stays.

I recommend taking a small screwdriver on all your rides: You might find it handy if your derailleurs—either front or rear—fall out of adjustment while you're riding.

The bolt that attaches the rear derailleur to the frame is the upper pivot bolt. In some older bikes the rear derailleur is still attached to the frame by means of a fixing plate or clamp. But most good bikes should have an integral ''ear'' brazed on to the dropout to attach the rear derailleur.

Maintenance on the rear derailleur is pretty straightforward. Clean it in soapy water with a large, soft brush every few hundred miles. After about fifteen thousand miles the rear derailleur rollers can become worn. If so, replace them with a new set. To remove the old set unfasten the bolt that holds the rollers to the cage plates. Remove the rollers and the bushings. To install the new rollers just reverse this operation.

As with the front derailleurs, the cable linking the rear derailleur to the shift lever may become stretched with time. To tighten it, simply loosen the cable clamp (usually with an eight-millimeter wrench) and tug at the cable with your fingers. When the cable is taut, fasten the cable clamp again. If this doesn't work use vise-grips to pull the cable taut. Just remember, wrap the cable in a *thick* towel, or you'll fray the cable end.

While your rear derailleur cable is loose, this is a good opportunity to check the cable housing that directs the cable from the rear derailleur to a braze-on on the chainstay. If your bike is new, the cable housing probably won't need lubrication. But if you've ridden a few thousand miles, take it off and spray it with WD-40 (a commonly available synthetic lubricant that doesn't break down as quickly as oil) or an equivalent Teflon spray.

If you fall over on your bike on the derailleur side, always check to see if your rear derailleur is all right. Because the unit does stick out, it can be the first component to be damaged. If you have any serious damage, get a new derailleur—most models are fairly inexpensive.

Rear derailleurs can become worn out with age. If yours simply doesn't respond very well anymore, consider either replacing the gear return spring or buying a new derailleur.

Freewheel

Next to the rear derailleur is the freewheel. The freewheel has a fairly complicated interior mechanism, and it should never be taken apart by nonprofessional mechanics. The most common maintenance on the freewheel is simply to clean the freewheel about every twenty-five hundred miles or so.

To clean the freewheel you will need to take it off the rear wheel. For this, you'll need a special freewheel remover designed for your specific freewheel. This is one area of cycling in which there's a tremendous degree of variation. Don't use something that's a near fit. You'll need a lot of force to remove the freewheel—pedaling will have tightened the freewheel forcefully at the hub—and a poor fit could bend the freewheel and the hub.

After removing the rear wheel from the frame, unfasten the quick release skewer and remove the skewer nut and spring. Attach the freewheel remover to the freewheel body. Make sure it's a snug, exact fit. Replace the skewer spring and nut and fasten the quick release skewer tightly.

Because the freewheel is tightened progressively as you ride, you'll need a big wrench, such as a twelve-inch adjustable wrench or a pair of large vise-grips, to remove the freewheel. Clamp the wrench of your choice on the flat of the freewheel remover. Hold the wheel firmly between your legs and push down. Be sure to push in a counterclockwise direction—otherwise you'll be tightening the freewheel.

In most cases it'll take a little brawn to loosen the freewheel. Make sure you put your body into it. The bigger your wrench, the more leverage you'll have: That'll make it easier to unfasten.

After you've loosened the freewheel, unfasten the quick release nut and unfasten the freewheel slowly either with the wrench or by hand. If the freewheel suddenly gets stuck, don't force it. Most likely, you've run up against some dirt in the threads attaching the freewheel to the hub. If you play with the freewheel, moving it gently back and forth, you can usually dislodge the dirt.

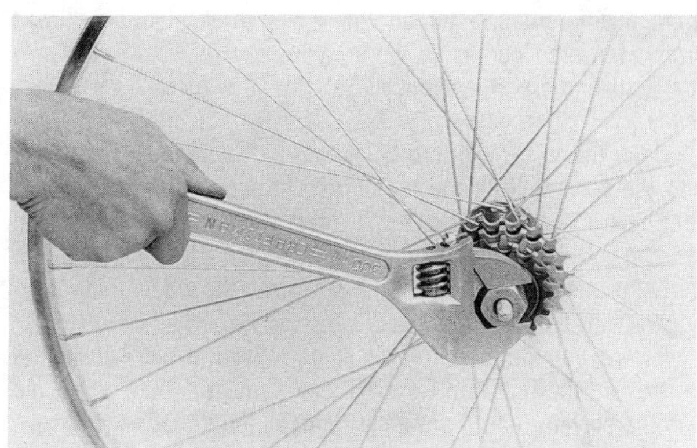

Removing the freewheel. Install the freewheel remover and loosen from hub with wrench. Note: Nearly every brand of freewheel has its own freewheel remover—make sure you have the right one.

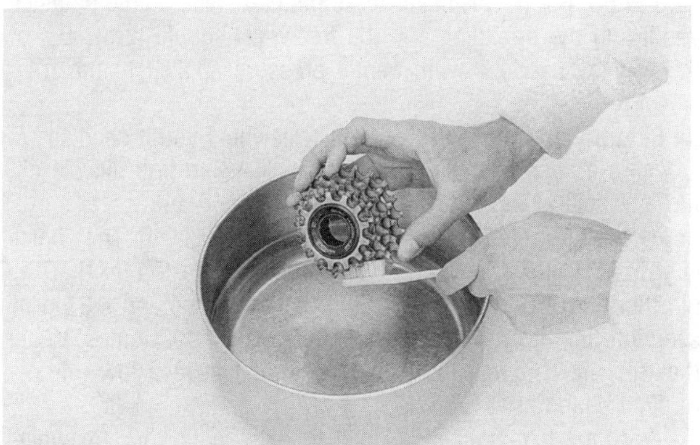

Cleaning the freewheel. Dip the freewheel into a bucket of solvent. Then dip an old toothbrush into the solvent and scrub off extra dirt.

If that doesn't work you might have damaged threads and may need to take the whole thing to a professional bike shop. They might be able to salvage your hub and freewheel if the damage is only superficial. If there's a lot of damage, they could grind a different size thread (there are three standard thread sizes). If worse comes to worst, you may have to get a new rear hub and freewheel body. But this is a pretty rare occurrence.

Once the freewheel is off, take an old toothbrush and dip it into the solvent. Run the toothbrush through all the sprockets. After the sprockets are cleaned, take the entire unit and dip it into the wire basket inside the can of solvent. Let it sit for about thirty seconds. When you take it out, rinse the whole thing thoroughly with a strong hose.

Before you put the freewheel back on the hub, clean the threads on the rear hub (to avoid any damage). Take a rag, dip it in the solvent, and thoroughly clean all the threads. Never use something like a bristle brush on the threads. They're fragile and a metal brush could damage them.

Put the freewheel back on the rear hub by hand, carefully. The crucial step is to find the threading. At first it may be a bit hard to do. But never, *never* force the unit. With a little patience you'll find the threading and the freewheel should turn most of the way by hand, or with gentle pressure applied to the freewheel remover.

Before you start riding on your freewheel you'll need to relubricate it. Use a medium-weight oil, like 3-in-One bicycle oil. It's available at most any hardware, bike, and auto parts store. Some people prefer a synthetic lubricant like WD-40. The choice is yours. Tip the freewheel with the outside on top so that the oil drips into the main body. Spin the freewheel and let the oil seep into the body. Repeat this about three or four times. When the freewheel is well lubricated, it should have a low, almost muffled sound as it turns.

Any time it rains, you'll need to relubricate your freewheel with a little 3-in-One oil. But if you ride in a lot of rain, you really should clean the freewheel before you add any more oil, because you might be riding with damaging dirt particles inside the main body.

Most advanced riders like to change the sprockets on their freewheels according to the kind of riding they're doing. This is relatively simple and requires only two cog or sprocket removers and extra cogs. While you need to buy the cogs specifically made for your freewheel model, the sprocket remover is a cheap, universal tool that's simply composed of a short piece of chain attached to a metal arm for leverage—you can even make your own with a few household tools.

You can leave the freewheel on the hub while changing the sprockets. You need to know, however, how your freewheel is designed. Many Japanese models are made with only one threaded outside sprocket; the other sprockets can be slid off. But most Regina freewheels (an Italian brand) have two sets of threads. The first set turns to the outside, and usually consists of the outside three sprockets. The two or three inside sprockets are removed from the inside.

Whatever the design of your freewheel, always begin with the outside sprocket—that's the smallest one. Wrap the first cog remover *clockwise* around this cog. Wrap the other cog remover counterclockwise on any other cog (the second-to-last one on the inside is my favorite because it's big enough to provide leverage and close enough to the outside cog for stability).

Using the second cog remover as an anchor, tug at the outside cog. Often the best way to do this is to put your whole body into it. Just like the freewheel itself, the cogs are tightened progressively as you ride—they could be pretty tight.

After you've loosened the outside cog, take it off and remove any spacer that might be placed between this outside cog and the following one. Spacers and cogs are very specific on freewheels and rarely interchangeable. Keep track of what came from where, or you could end up rebuilding your freewheel incorrectly and jamming your chain.

Remove all the cogs you need to change according to the type of freewheel you have. When you get replacements, though, make sure you know exactly where you want them on the freewheel. On a Maillard freewheel, for example, a seventeen-tooth cog on the inside is entirely different from a seventeen-tooth cog three sprockets from the inside. Ask your dealer to provide you with assistance if you need it.

When you've replaced the cogs or the freewheel itself, you may feel a kind of lurching, as if the freewheel is loose for the first revolution or so. Very simply, that's because the freewheel *is* loose when you first put it on. As you ride on it it will tighten. This is nothing to worry about.

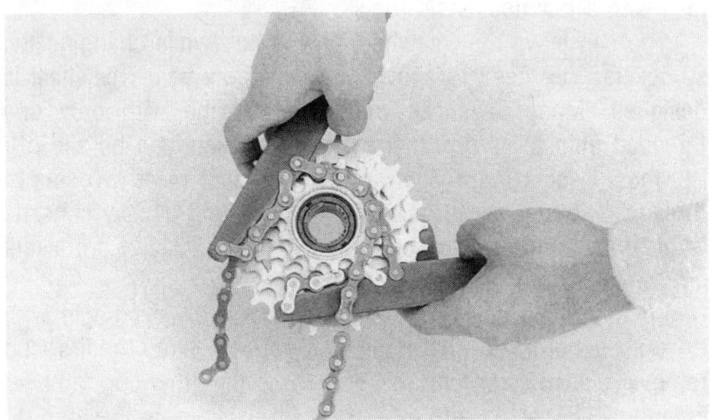

Removing freewheel sprockets. Use two sprocket removers. In this example the freewheel is off the bike for ease of illustration. But when you do it, you should leave your freewheel on the bike.

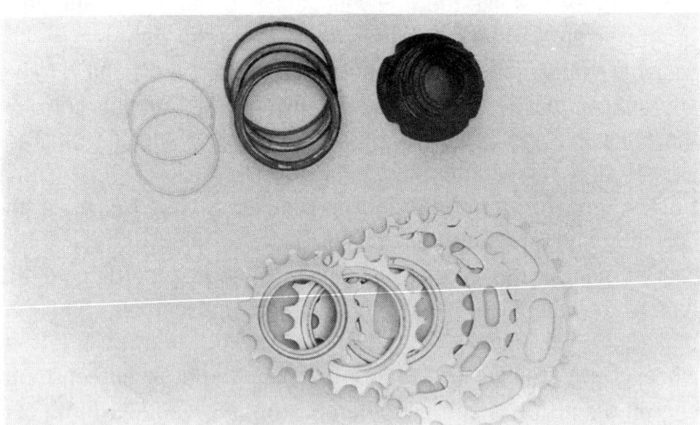

A disassembled freewheel. Note the spacers and the different sizes of the sprocket threads. Always be very careful to correctly reassemble your freewheel with the right sprockets and spacers.

Chain

Connecting the entire drivetrain is the primitive transmission called the chain. The chain was invented in the 1870s and hasn't changed much since then (although the links have become half as big as they used to be in the old days).

The chain requires more frequent maintenance than any other part of the bike. Every hundred miles or so, you should lubricate the chain. To do this, turn the pedals backward and pour a medium-weight oil like 3-in-One for about fifteen seconds. As you do this, you'll notice some oil dripping onto your chainstay. Just clean that up with some of the solvent and wipe it dry with a paper towel.

Every thousand miles or so (or sooner if you've been riding in wet weather) you'll need to overhaul your chain. To do this, take your chain tool and open any one of the links on the chain by popping out any one of the rivets. This is an easy tool to use, but make sure you use it with care. Otherwise you could damage one of the chain plates and find yourself short one chain link (which often means buying a new chain—more of a hassle than it seems, as I explain below).

With the link open, thread the chain gently through the drivetrain, making sure you're holding the end with the open rivet. It's too wide to fit through the derailleurs. Take the chain gently by both ends, but be careful not to wrap it—you might have trouble unwrapping it.

Dip the chain into the solvent and let it sit for about a minute. When you remove it, remove any excess filth by rubbing all the links carefully with a toothbrush dipped in the solvent. As always when you use solvent, rinse the chain thoroughly using a powerful hose.

To put the chain back on the drivetrain, simply thread it through again. Make sure the open rivet with the cylinder that's sticking out is facing you, or you'll have a tough time closing it. Start with the end that has the open rivet and thread the chain through the chainrings, through the front derailleur, and back to the rear derailleur. Both ends should meet at the bottom, between the rear derailleur and the crankset.

Close the rivet with the chain tool, holding the chain plates together while gently forcing the rivet back through the plates. When the rivet looks flush with both plates, you can remove the chain tool. In most cases, though, the newly closed rivet will be tight. Take the tight link and a neighboring link in your hands and gently sway them up and down and in and out. After a few seconds, the rivet will be loose. (If you ever develop a tight link in normal riding, you should try this same procedure.)

The most common chain problem is age. As chains get old they stretch out and should be replaced. Every fifteen thousand miles or so you should automatically replace your chain. The only problem with this is that as the chain has aged it has also worn out the cogs in your freewheel and the chainrings.

Ideally, every time you buy a new chain you should buy new freewheel cogs and chainrings. If you don't, you'll find that the chain will skip on the cogs and chainrings because it won't be perfectly matched. Of course, most people can't invest in so much new hardware all at once. And if the cogs have only been slightly worn out, the chain will stretch out soon enough. But you should never use freewheel cogs or chainrings for more than three chain changes—if you do, your chain could skip continually.

Brakes

Brakes are your primary safety valve and should be perfectly maintained. Luckily, the bicycle caliper brake is much simpler than an automobile disk or drum brake. It's also much easier to maintain.

The main body of the brake is composed of the calipers. They are virtually maintenance-free. Simply make sure you wash them in soapy water every few hundred miles or so, or more often if you ride in a lot of dirt or rain. The vast majority of brakes today are side-pull brakes. These brakes have two-part bodies, a larger unit that includes the arm extending up to the cable housing and a smaller unit that includes the caliper below the arm. If you have center-pull brakes, the construction is a little more complicated but just as easy to maintain.

Perhaps the main difference with center-pulls is that these have an extra link in the system, a piece of cable that links both calipers. That piece of cable is then attached to a cup, which in turn is attached to the main brake cable, which runs back to the brake lever.

The most common headaches with brakes are poor adjustments. You'll probably find that your brakes pull to one side, leaving one of the brake pads rubbing on the rim below the tire. To remedy this problem, you'll need a special narrow cross-section wrench (often a thirteen-millimeter size). You can use the same wrench you use to remove your pedals. Some high-quality brakes have a recessed allen head behind the fork crown that allows you to adjust the lateral position of the brakes with an allen wrench.

To adjust the lateral position of the brake in relation to the wheel, fit the narrow cross-section wrench into the flat on the brake axle right before the fork crown (for the front brake) or right before the brake bridge (for the rear brake). Turn the wrench to center the brake. Of course, if you have a recessed head behind the fork crown (or the brake bridge), then adjust the brake back there.

You'll have to go beyond perfect center. To test if you've centered the brakes just right, hit the brake levers on the handlebars once. After you hit the brakes they will pop back to a certain position. That's where your adjustment has left them—you may have to repeat this operation a few more times before you get it just right.

With use, brake cables tend to stretch out. If this starts happening, you'll find the travel of your brake lever increased and your effective braking force reduced. Luckily, most manufacturers have an adjustable barrel that can be turned to take up the slack in the cable. In many brakes, this barrel is placed at the top of the brake arm where the cable housing starts. Other designs have this barrel next to the bolt that fastens the cable to the brake, a little bit lower down. If you have center-pull brakes, you'll find your adjustable barrel in the special washer that's fitted into the head tube.

Of course, if you've gone as far as you can with the adjustable barrel, you'll need to tighten the brake cable. To do this, unfasten the bolt that holds the brake cable (usually with an eight-millimeter wrench). As the cable is released, the spring held by the brake calipers will open up the brake.

To tighten your brake, take one hand, pass it through the spokes on the wheel, and hold both brake shoes firmly against the rim of the bike. With the other hand, tug firmly at the brake cable to make sure it is taut. Then let go of the cable and tighten the bolt (keep holding the brake shoes tightly until the cable bolt is completely tightened). As you let go of the brake shoes, the calipers will be released just enough to give you sufficient clearance between the brake shoes and the rim.

If you have a very old cable, I would recommend getting new cables, something you should do anyway every five thousand miles or six months. To remove the old brake cable, repeat the procedure described above, loosen the brake cable and slip it out of the brake body. Then grab the plastic cable housing and pull it off. Leave it aside for the time being.

Your brake lever will be loose, no longer restrained by the pressure of the cable attached to the brake. You can open it wide to remove the large cable barrel end from the barrel lock inside the brake lever. The brake cable will probably be hard to remove, so use a screwdriver to lightly tap it out.

Make sure the new brake cable you purchase has the same barrel end as the one you're replacing. There are a number of different brake barrel designs and they are not compatible. Also, when you're buying a new cable try to get the thickest cable available for your model. Campagnolo makes an especially thick brake cable that can be used on a lot of the ''Campagnolo clone'' brakes. It's a little more expensive but more than worth the price in added safety.

To install the new brake cable, slot the barrel end through the barrel lock in the brake lever. Some models have an open slot in the barrel lock, allowing you to pass the cable through the barrel lock before pulling on the cable to fit the barrel end. But some models have a closed barrel lock, which means you'll have to thread the entire cable through the barrel lock.

Once the barrel end is in place in the barrel lock, give the cable a firm tug to make sure it won't pop out. Since there is no tension on your cable yet, the barrel end could still slide out. You'll need to check it again before you tighten the cable to the brake body.

Grease the cable and thread it through the housing. Then thread the cable through the brake, tighten the calipers by holding the brake shoes against the rim, as described above. Tighten the bolt. Make sure the barrel end is firmly inside the barrel lock of the brake lever as you tighten the cable.

Because replacement brake cables come in standard lengths only, you'll need to clip off the excess cable with a wire cutter. Take special care when cutting the end of your cable—if you fray it, you'll have to get a new cable. Some people like to put plastic plugs on the ends of their brake cables, but this isn't necessary.

There is one special case in changing brake cables. If you have aerodynamic cable housing that runs through the bars, you won't be able to remove the cable housing. Instead, you'll have to painstakingly thread the cable through the housing.

Every fifteen thousand miles you should change the cable housing. Purchase one length of high-quality housing that will accommodate both your front and rear brakes. Make sure to buy more than you need to account for any mistakes. Start with the rear brake. Remove the brake cable as described above. Then remove the housing. On most bikes you'll have brazed-on mounts holding the cable housing to the top tube. Simply slip the housing out through these mounts. If you have screwed-on clips, you'll need to get a small screwdriver to unfasten the screws.

Take your new cable housing in one hand and let it hang. Take the old cable housing in the other hand and let it hang too. Mark the length you need on your new cable housing by making an indentation with your nail on the plastic. Then take a pair of wire cutters and cut the new cable housing. Take great care not to fray the housing, by always cutting in a line perpendicular to the swirl of the metallic housing inside the plastic casing.

Install the new housing, thread the cable through it, and you're set. Repeat the same steps with the front housing. Watch for housing that's too short or too long. You always want the housing to form a gentle, graceful loop above the handlebars that will be easy for the cable to run through. If the housing gets short, you'll get an abrupt curve. That will restrict the cable's ability to pull the brakes. If the housing is too long, it'll require an overly long section of brake cable, which will make for less efficient braking.

Every fifteen thousand miles or so you should change your brake pads. To do this, take a wrench (again, usually an eight-millimeter model) and unfasten the bolts that hold the brake shoe and pad to the main brake assembly.

Once the bolts are loose, take the brake shoe and turn it a few degrees with the rear of the brake shoe facing down. Tighten. Then take a large screwdriver and gently force the old brake pad out of the brake shoe—it'll slide out slowly.

To install the new brake pad, unfasten the brake shoe and turn it so now the *front* is facing down. Tighten the brake shoe. Wedge the brake pad into the beginning of the brake shoe and

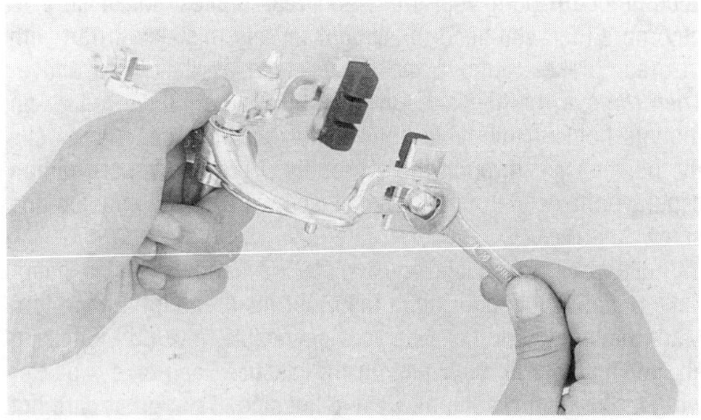

Unfastening the brake shoe. Use a wrench to loosen the bolt and remove the brake shoe.

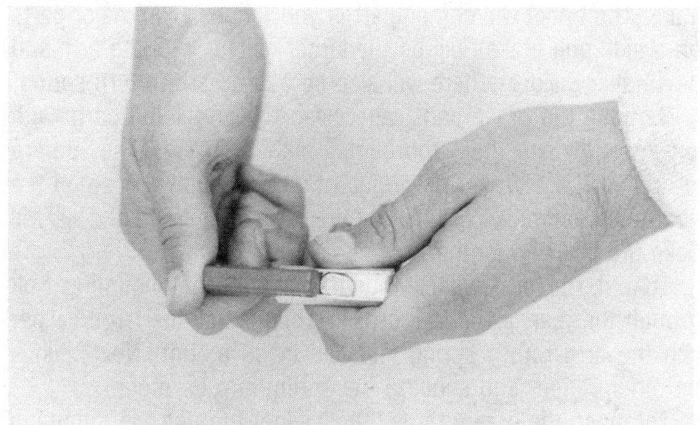

Installing a new brake pad. You can push a new brake shoe in by hand, but you may want to use a screwdriver. To remove an old brake pad you will definitely need a screwdriver.

push gently with the screwdriver until it's all the way in the brake shoe.

When you refasten the brake shoe, make sure it is parallel with the rim of the wheel.

Every fifteen thousand miles you should remove your brake to make an overhaul. Before you can make an overhaul, make sure the brake cables have been unfastened. Then, to remove the brake, you must anchor the axle. To do this take a wrench (often an eight-millimeter model) and place it on the nut at the front of the brake axle (more commonly known as the *mounting bolt*). On many modern side-pulls you can place an allen key in the recessed bolt behind the fork crown to make it easier to unfasten the nut at the front of the mounting bolt.

Then take a wrench (either an eight-millimeter wrench or an allen key in most cases) and loosen the nut on the front end of the brakes. After removing the nut, you can unfasten the washer that sits right behind the nut. This washer may require a wrench to remove it (usually a ten-millimeter model).

Once the washer is removed, you can take out the mounting bolt (or brake axle). The mounting bolt will slide back, off the brake. The brake will come apart in your hands. The major parts (on a side-pull brake) will be the larger caliper with the arm and the smaller caliper. There will also be a large arm return spring.

Remove the brake pads, and clean the remaining parts with solvent and rinse them thoroughly with a strong hose. Before you reinstall the brake, put a dab of white lithium grease on the mounts on the brake calipers where the spring is held. This will make the brake smoother.

To put the brake back together, install the mounting bolt through the rear of the fork crown. Then install the large caliper with the arm return spring installed in its mount. Next, install the other caliper and squeeze the spring into its mount.

To attach the brake, thread the washer through the mounting bolt. Turn it to the point at which there is no more play on the mounting bolt. Next you'll need to hold the *washer* tightly with a wrench as you tighten the mounting bolt *nut* with the other wrench. After you tighten the nut you'll notice the brake will be a little stiff. Then take the washer and *loosen* it a eighth of a turn or so. This will loosen your brake and also tighten the nut, making your brake safer.

If you want to readjust or change your brake levers, you'll need to take out the brake cable and remove all the tape from the handlebars. Then you'll need to open the levers as far as they'll go and use a wrench (again, usually an eight-millimeter model) and unfasten the bolt at the back, inside the lever assembly.

Once the bolt is loose, the clamp surrounding the handlebars may still stick. In that case, lightly tap the bolt you just unfastened. With the clamp loose, you can move the brake lever. If you're adjusting the position, remember, the ideal spot is about halfway down the bend on the handlebars—at that point the *bottom* of the levers should be just about level with the bottom of the bars.

You may want to change the rubber brake hood that surrounds the brake lever assembly. First you must remove the brake lever as described above. Then take the old hood and squeeze it off from the rear. To install the new hood, install it also from the rear. You'll need a little muscle. But make sure you don't stretch the hood at the front where it is thin—you'll split it.

To reinstall the levers, simply tighten the bolt in the assembly. Make sure the brake levers face directly in front of you.

Handlebars

To remove your handlebars, take off the tape and the levers. Then loosen the bolt in the stem that holds the bars. Once that bolt is loose, simply move the bars out. When the bend in the bars crosses the stem, you'll have to be a little careful. Make sure you don't scuff the bars.

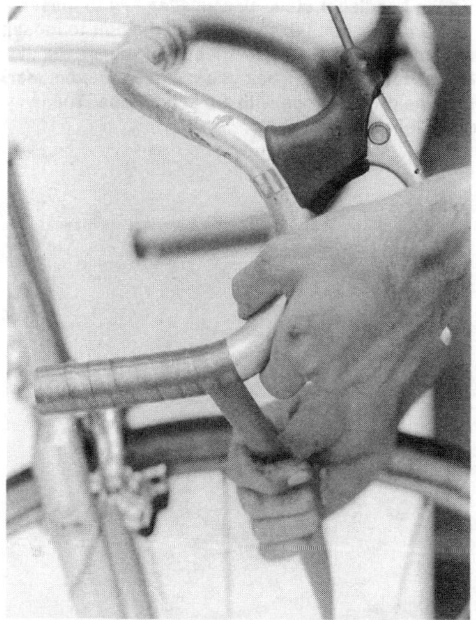

Installing new tape on the handlebars. Start at the bottom and apply tape firmly, making sure to have a little overlap on each turn.

Handlebar Stem

The stem should be removed every five thousand miles to make sure the expander wedge inside the steering tube (which is inside the head tube) doesn't ''freeze.'' If this expander wedge does freeze, it'll never come out and you'll have to go to a bike shop to have the expander wedge cracked and removed.

To remove the expander wedge, unfasten the bolt at the top of the stem and take out the stem. Then take a dollop of white lithium grease and put it around the expander wedge. Reinstall the stem. When you tighten the stem, make sure it is tight, but don't force it too tight, or you'll crack the expander wedge.

Removing the handlebar stem. Use an allen key to loosen the bolt. In some cases, you may need to tap the bolt to loosen the expander wedge inside the stem. Clean and grease the expander wedge before reinstalling. When you remove the stem mark the spot where the grease stops with a piece of tape. That way you can reinstall it in the right spot.

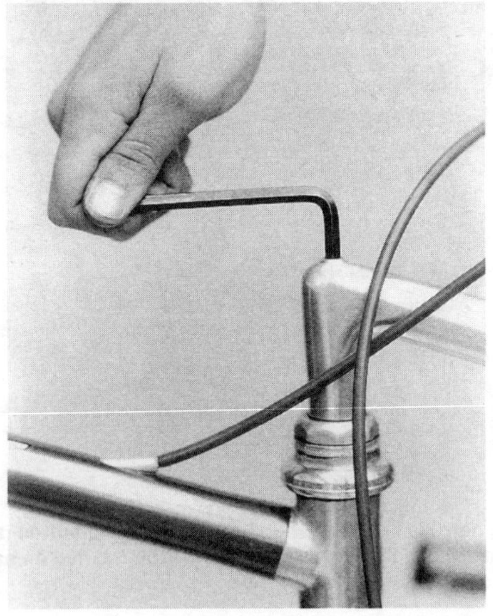

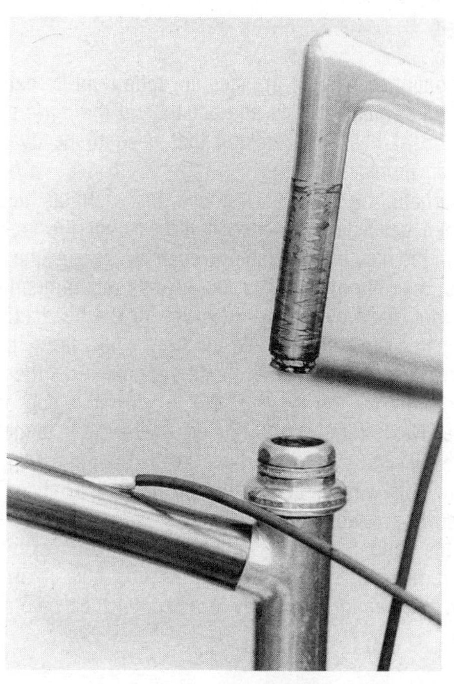

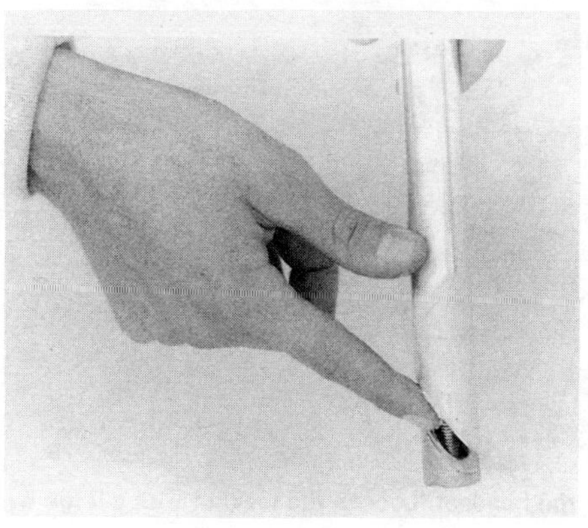

Headset

The component that holds the steering tube (and its extension, the fork) is the headset. Like the pedals and the bottom bracket, the headset has ball bearings that need to be overhauled every fifteen thousand miles.

To overhaul the headset, remove the stem as described above. Then get a large wrench that'll fit over the locknut. A twelve-inch monkey or adjustable wrench will fit over the locknut on the vast majority of headsets, but I would recommend getting a special tool made by the manufacturer of the headset.

To unfasten the locknut, hold the front wheel firmly between your legs to anchor the fork and steering tube. Give the wrench a yank and remove the locknut. Put it aside in a cup or other safe place. Next, remove the tanged washer (the tange is the little piece that sticks into a groove in the steering tube). Most of the time this washer comes out by hand. If it sticks take a medium-sized screwdriver and pop it up gently.

With the tanged washer removed, take your wrench and carefully remove the screwed race. As you take it off, you'll notice the ball bearings—usually in a race of their own.

Removing the headset. Loosen the locknut with a large wrench.

Remove the screwed race.

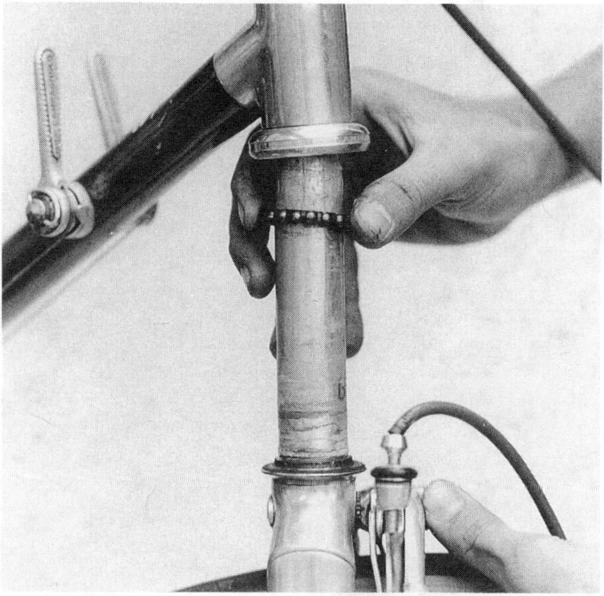

After placing the screwed race in a safe place, remove the forks and steering tube.

With the screwed race loose, the steering tube will fall out of the head tube and expose the bottom set of ball bearings, which are lodged in what's known as the *crown race.*

Take the ball bearings and dip them into the wire basket that fits in the can of solvent. Let them sit. Then take a soft cloth or rag, dip it in the solvent, and wipe the grooves in the large races. Before reinstalling the headset, rinse everything thoroughly with a strong hose.

To reinstall the headset, first apply white lithium grease on all the races and ball bearings. Slip the bottom set of ball bearings on the steering tube all the way to the crown race. Then slip the steering tube back into the head tube.

Next, slip the top set of ball bearings and place it on the top

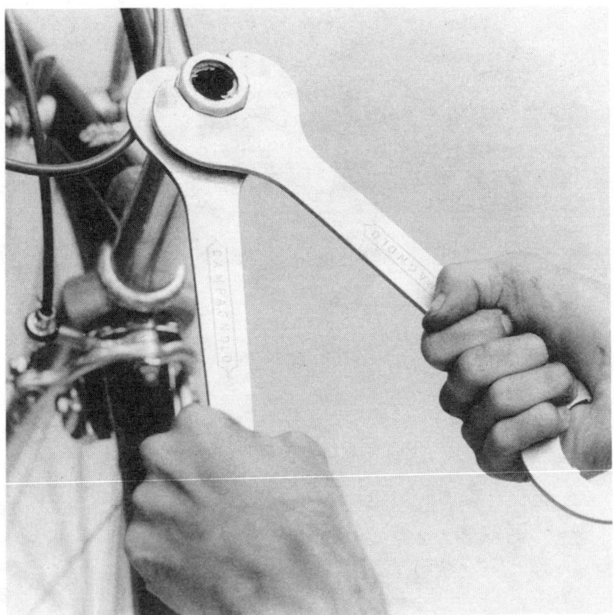

To tighten the locknut, you need one wrench to anchor the screwed race, the other to tighten the locknut.

pressed race. To attach the steering tube, thread the screwed race up to the ball bearings until there is no more play but before you can feel any roughness. Then reinstall the tanged washer.

When you reinstall the locknut, make sure that you have a wrench to anchor the screwed race. Slowly tighten the locknut, making sure to keep the bottom wrench around the screwed race stationary. When you're satisfied that the locknut is tight, *loosen* the screwed race an eighth of a turn or so until it's not rough.

Before reinstalling your stem, check for any play in the headset. Play in the headset is especially dangerous because you can easily break the steering tube, causing a serious accident.

If you have trouble completing this overhaul, see a professional mechanic—he'll be able to help you in a matter of minutes.

Seat and Seat Post

The seat post should be removed every fifteen thousand miles and the portion inside the frame should be lightly greased with white lithium grease. Whenever you remove the seat post, take a piece of tape to mark exactly the point where the seat post meets the frame. Remember, finding the right position is a painstaking process. You don't want to lose it when you remove your seat post.

The saddle doesn't require any special maintenance, but you may want to remove it once in a while to clean the railing underneath the seat. To remove the saddle from the seat post, get a wrench appropriate to the seat post you have. In many cases this will require an allen key and the saddle will be easy to remove. But some Campagnolo models have two conventional twelve-millimeter bolts that require a special wrench to reach them without a lot of trouble.

When you remove the saddle, be sure to mark the point on the railing where the saddle was positioned. Remember, this is an important part of your position. If you reinstall the saddle incorrectly along the railing, you'll be riding in the wrong position.

Wheels

Wheels are a very important part of your bike. They should be maintained with a great deal of care. The wheels are your primary point of contact with the road. If they're poorly adjusted they will make your riding inefficient, and possibly dangerous.

Although some cycling books outline wheel building, I don't recommend it for anybody who isn't an advanced mechanic. To build a really good wheel requires a range of expensive tools and, more than anything else, much skill and experience. Most wheels that are built by riders in their homes tend to be poorly built.

The hardest thing about building a good wheel is knowing just how to tighten the spokes. While it's pretty easy to form a wheel, chances are that your spokes will be very unevenly tightened. This kind of wheel falls out of true very often and puts a lot of stress on the spokes and rims. Because it's so hard to tighten all the spokes evenly, many homemade wheels are not round. And that puts even more stress on the wheel. And keep in mind that the wheel is made of fragile components, like thin spokes and rims, that are only strong and safe when put together in the right way.

Get your wheels built by a professional. If you do, you'll notice that you'll need to spend much less time adjusting and readjusting. You'll have many fewer broken spokes. Most of all, your bike will be a heck of a lot safer.

Of course, even with well-made wheels, you'll need to know how to do some of your own maintenance. Because they have ball bearings, the hubs should be overhauled every fifteen thousand miles, more often if you ride in much bad weather or dirt.

If you have Mavic, Shimano, or any other kind of sealed-bearing hubs, you won't need to do any maintenance. These hubs are maintenance-free and only need to be washed in warm, soapy water every few hundred miles.

To overhaul your hubs, remove the wheel from the bike. Remove the freewheel from the rear hub as described on pages 94—98. Take out the quick release skewer. Before you set it

After removing the wheel from the frame, remove the quick-release skewer if your bike has one.

aside, make sure you put the little springs back on the skewer and tighten the nut on the end to make sure they don't get lost. Set the quick release skewers aside.

Next, unfasten the hub axles. To do this, turn the wheel on its side. Take two cone wrenches, the same kind of narrow cross-section wrenches you used to unfasten your pedals and adjust your brakes.

Take the first cone wrench and place it on the inner cone, just outside the edge of the hub body. Take the other wrench and place it around the locknut, which is on the end of the axle.

Use the first wrench to *anchor* the inner cone while you unfasten the locknut with the second wrench. Once the locknut is loose, unthread it and set it aside in a small cup. Next, unthread the inner cone slowly and set it aside.

Once the locknut and inner cone are off, you can slip off the hub axle. Set it aside. To remove the bearings, pop off the dust cap that sits at the edge of the hub body. With the vast majority of hubs, you simply need to take a medium-sized screwdriver and gently pop the dust cap out. But if you have the new Campagnolo Aero Record hubs, you'll need a special tool produced by Campagnolo to take off the dust caps.

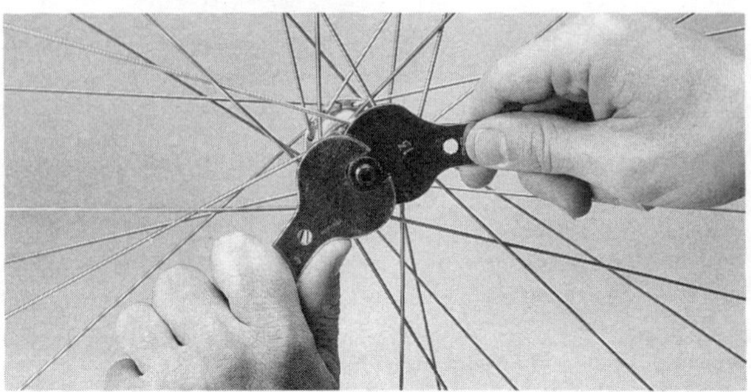

To remove the cone from the hub, apply a cone wrench to the inner cone as an anchor. Then apply the second cone wrench to the outer cone, loosen, and remove. Now you can remove the inner cone.

From the other side of the hub, grab the axle (there is no need to remove the cones from this side of the axle).

Remove the axle from the hub.

Apply a screwdriver to pop the dust cap from the hub body so that you can get at the ball bearings.

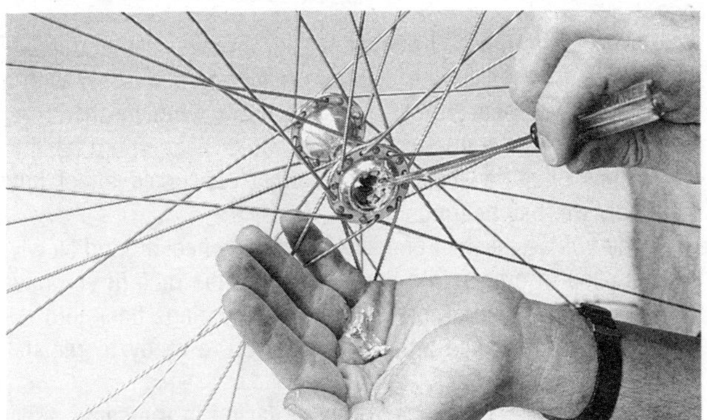

Finally, using the screwdriver, remove the ball bearings (or bearings race if the bearings are in one) from the hub. Repeat the process for the other side. Now the hub and bearings are ready to be cleaned with solvent, dried, and regreased.

Once the dust caps are off, you'll be able to take out the ball bearings. If your ball bearings are in a track (a race), simply lift the whole thing out. If your ball bearings are free, take them out (carefully) by hand. You may need a screwdriver or tweezers to help you. Put the ball bearings, the race (if you have one), and the dust cap in the wire basket inside the solvent. Let it sit.

To remove the ball bearings from the other side, simply flip the wheel over, remove the dust cap and repeat the same operation.

Once everything is sitting in the wire basket in the solvent, take a soft cloth or rag, dip it into the solvent and clean out the grease in the groove in the hub where the ball bearings sit. Wash out the solvent in the hub with a powerful hose.

Once you've done that, take the wire basket out of the solvent can and spray all the parts inside the wire basket with the hose. You're now ready to start reinstalling all the parts.

The first step is to take a liberal dollop of grease and pack it in the grooves in the hubs where the ball bearings sit. Then take one race of ball bearings and dip it into the grease as well. If you don't have races, simply reinstall the bearings one by one.

Once you've finished one side, take the dust cap and *lightly* tap it back into place with a rubber mallet or a hammer with a thick cloth wrapped around it. If you don't wrap the hammer, you might warp the dust cap, which would mean you'd have to get a new one, because a warped dust cap could affect how smoothly the ball bearings turn.

Once you've finished one side, turn the wheel around slowly. Put a dollop of grease into the groove. Dip the race (if you have one) into the grease. Then pack the ball bearings back into the hub. Tap the dust cap into place and you're ready to reinstall the hub axle.

Always be sure to place your axle facing in the same direction you took it out. The spacers on the axle and the fine-tuned adjustment of the wheel were done with the axle facing in a specific direction. This is especially true with the rear axle.

Once the axle is back in place, thread the inner cone until you feel no more play on the axle. Then hold both ends of the axle in your hands and spin the wheel. If you feel any roughness, loosen the inner cone. The ideal point is that at which there is no more side-to-side play and no more roughness as the wheel turns.

Then rethread the locknut, slowly. Wrap one cone wrench around this locknut and another around the locknut on the *other* side of the hub (the one you never removed). This will anchor the axle as you thread the locknut.

Once the locknut is barely touching the inner cone, place the second cone wrench on the inner cone. Use that cone wrench as an anchor so the inner cone doesn't fall out of position.

Tighten the locknut, but make sure that the inner cone doesn't budge: If it does, the whole thing will be too tight, and you'll be grinding ball bearings. Once you're satisfied that the locknut is tight (and it really *has* to be tight), take the inner cone and *loosen* it a quarter turn. You need to do this because even the steadiest hand can't keep the inner cone from tightening a little bit while the locknut is tightened.

Some people have trouble with this. They find that when they tighten the locknut, the inner cone tightens way too much. A trick you can use to avoid this is to leave the inner cone just a little looser before you tighten the locknut. But don't leave it too loose, or you'll end up having a lot of play on the hub.

If you have any damage to the hub or axle, you should take the wheel to a professional mechanic to ask his opinion on how to repair it.

The spokes are really the key structural element of the wheels. Although each spoke is very thin and light, it has a tremendous tensile strength. And put all together in a crossover pattern, the spokes form a very strong wheel.

Because a tremendous amount of stress is placed on the spokes, spokes sometimes become loose. To tighten a spoke, take a spoke wrench and tighten the nipple that attaches the spoke to the rim.

Be careful, however, because the tension of the spoke determines the structure (roundness, strength) of the wheel. Turn the nipple until it starts to create a little resistance. Then turn an eighth of a turn at a time, making sure the wheel is true as you tighten the spoke. The best way to make sure the wheel is true is to install it in a truing stand as you work. Chances are you don't own your own truing stand, but some good bike shops will have one available for their customers to use. If you can't find a truing stand, one acceptable solution is to put your wheel back on your bike and use the brake pads as a guide—but this is a very rough measure.

One note of caution: If your wheel is perfectly trued with one spoke very loose, your wheel is probably improperly built. In this case I would recommend taking it to a professional wheel builder to see if he can readjust it for you.

If you're wondering what's so bad about a wheel that's perfectly trued minus one spoke, the answer is very simple: You'll have a wheel built with an odd number of spokes, with more pull to one side than the other: You're always going to have spokes coming loose or breaking.

If you have a broken spoke, replace it immediately. The first step is to get the *exact* same length spoke. To determine exact spoke length, you need to know what brand of hub you have, and whether your hub is low-flange or high-flange. You need to know in what pattern your spokes are arranged. Most bikes have three-or four-across spoke patterns. (What this refers to is how many times each spoke crosses another.) To find out what pattern your spokes have, choose any spoke. Start at the hub and count how many spokes it crosses. This will give you the pattern.

Next you need to know what brand and type of rim you have. If you have clincher (or wired-on) wheels, you'll have a slightly different spoke than with a sew-up (or tubular) wheel. Finally, you need to know whether the broken spoke is on the front wheel or the rear wheel.

Armed with all that information, you can go to your bike shop. When you get your replacement spokes, you might as well buy a few more—they're inexpensive and good to have around your workshop.

To remove the broken spoke, remove the wheel from the bike, then deflate your tire and remove it. If you have clincher (or wired-on) wheels, you'll need to take a tire iron and pop the rubber tire out of the rim. With a second tire iron, slowly pull the rest of the tire out of the rim. Then turn the wheel around, take one tire iron and scoop the tire out of the rim. Then, with the second tire iron (and possibly a third) remove the rest of the tire. As you get almost all the way done, you'll notice it'll become hard to remove the last bit of tire. Use a little muscle and you'll succeed. Once the tire is removed, take off the inner tube.

If you have sew-ups, make sure the tire is deflated. Turn the wheel so that the valve is resting squarely on the floor. Then start to dislodge the tire from the rim at the top of the wheel, directly opposite from the valve. With a little muscle the tire will come off the rim. When you get near the valve, turn the wheel so the valve is facing up and dislodge the tire up to the valve. Remove the tire.

With the tire off you can remove the portion of the spoke attached to the nipple. Gently ease it through the hole in the rim, up away from the hub of the wheel. If you have sew-up rims, you could have some glue buildup. By pushing a little harder on the spoke, you should be able to get the nipple and spoke through the spoke hole in the rim.

Now remove the bottom part of the spoke by threading it through the spoke hole on the hub. As you're doing this, you'll notice that there are two kinds of spoke holes on the hub.

If you have a damaged spoke that is in one piece, take your wire cutters and cut the spoke in half. You can't simply unthread

Replacing a spoke. After discarding the damaged spoke, carefully thread the new spoke through the hole in the freewheel flange. You will need to route through the spokes before inserting through the rim.

the nipple from the spoke because the spoke is so long that it won't fit through the maze of spokes once it's loosened.

Installing the new spoke presents the same problem. Because, obviously, you can't cut the new spoke, you'll need to first pull it all the way through the spoke hole on the hub. Make sure you are installing it in the right direction. You can tell which way is correct because each hole has an indentation. If you're installing a spoke that faces out, you'll have an easier time getting the spoke through, but you'll still have to bend it to get it through the spokes it has to cross.

To get the spoke up to the spoke hole on the rim, you'll have to cross it, usually three or four times. Look at the spoke pattern *two* spokes over on the same side of the wheel and follow that pattern meticulously.

Once you've finished crossing the spokes, which can take as long as ten or fifteen minutes, you'll need to bend the spoke slightly to get it into the spoke hole. Thread the nipple and tighten it with the spoke wrench up to the point at which you feel some resistance.

Once you feel some resistance, turn the spoke wrench one eighth of a turn at a time and check the true on the wheel. Again, you should do this in a truing stand. If you don't have one, look for a bike store that will let you use one. As a last resort, put the wheel back in the bike and use the brake pads as a rough guide.

Once you're satisfied the wheel is true (and round) you're done and you can put it back on your bike.

I think it's safe to say this is a pretty complicated procedure. And you're only changing one spoke. If you have to do a major repair, like a damaged or broken rim or hub, you need to rebuild an entire wheel. As I mentioned above, if you need your wheel rebuilt, you should look for an expert wheel builder—it's a very special skill that's well worth the money you're going to spend. Also, if somebody is rebuilding your wheel, it's really not worth it to skimp. Don't try to repair a broken rim, get a new one. And never use old spokes, they get stretched out in a specific pattern with each wheel: Buy new spokes. Last, if a few of your

Inserting a spoke nipple. Place it through the hole in the rim and thread it onto the spoke.

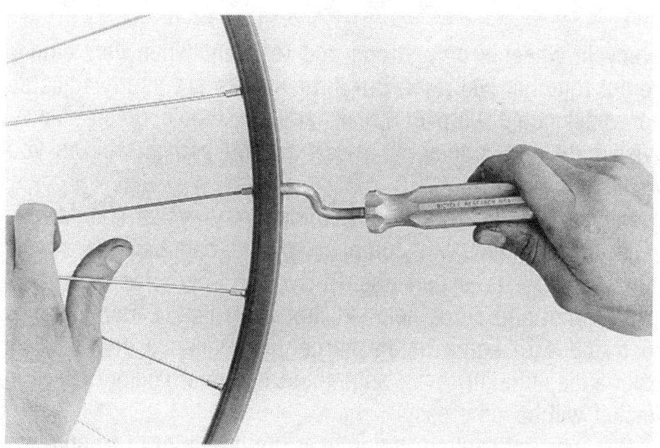

This spoke wrench tightens the spoke from the top of the nipple.

spokes seem loose, I suggest taking the wheel to a bicycle shop to have them true the wheels. Wheels will have to be trued more frequently if you ride a great deal on pot-holed city streets.

Remember, your wheels must be strong and resistant, even though the elements that make them up are extremely delicate.

This wrench is more common. It tightens the spoke through the body of the nipple.

A bicycle wheel is only strong and resistant when its elements are put together just right. But if the spokes are poorly adjusted, the wheel could warp or break, and you could crash. Always lavish care and money, as much as you can afford, on your wheels.

Bicycle maintenance is something every cyclist should master. It's really not that complicated and can become second nature with a little experience. But you will need the right tools, a little time, and some help. At first you might become terribly frustrated with some of the harder maintenance chores. With experience, though, even something like overhauling a bottom bracket will become easy.

One word of caution: If you ever run into a lot of trouble with a repair, never force anything. If, for example, you're trying to take off your freewheel, and you get stuck, forcing it will only ruin the threads, and therefore, both the freewheel and the hub.

Don't be ashamed if you run into a problem. Just take it down to your local bike shop and have a mechanic help you. I think you'll find most mechanics sympathetic. And they might be able to teach you a trade trick or two.

Some cyclists develop a tremendous interest in their equipment and eventually become top mechanics. They learn how to build and repair their frames and wheels. Eventually some become professional mechanics and frame builders. But unless you have the interest and determination to learn about your equipment, I would stick with the maintenance described here. If you ever have a more serious problem, go to a pro bike mechanic.

Greg LeMond's Complete Book of Bicycling
by Greg LeMond and Kent Gordis
illustrated with over 100 photographs

Greg LeMond, winner of the 1981 and 1985 Coors Classic, the 1983 World Championships, and the 1986 and 1989 Tours de France, is regarded as the top professional cyclist in the world. In his complete book on bicycling LeMond shows how millions of bicyclists in America can become better riders and get more enjoyment from the sport.

Greg Lemond's Complete Book of Bicycling describes and explains everything you need to know about buying, riding, and maintaining a bike, whether you are a recreational rider or a serious racer. Illustrated with over 100 instructive photos, the book discusses determining the proper frame size, how to select the best bike for the best value, what to avoid in buying a bike, seat and handlebar height, safety tips, and much more. LeMond discloses the training techniques that have helped make him the top cyclist in the world and even includes chapters on bicycle maintenance and a brief history of bicycling.

Liberally sprinkled with anecdotes from LeMond's own cycling experiences, this is *the* complete book on bicycling by the hottest cyclist in the world.

	PRICE	
	U.S.	CANADA
GREG LEMOND'S COMPLETE BOOK OF BICYCLING	$9.95	$12.95

Subtotal $ _______________

*Postage & handling $ _______________

Sales Tax $ _______________
(CA, NJ, NY, PA)

*Postage & handling:
$1.00 for 1 book,
25¢ for each
additional book up to
a maximum of $3.50

Total Amount Due $ _______________
Payable in U.S.
Funds (No cash
orders accepted)

Enclosed is my   ☐ check ☐ money order
Please charge my ☐ Visa ☐ MasterCard

Card # _________________________ Expiration Date _________

Signature as on charge card _______________________________

Name ____

Address ____

City _________________ State _________ Zip _________

Please allow six weeks for delivery. Prices subject to change
without notice.

17